Praise for *It Makes Sense!*...

It Makes Sense! Using the Hundreds Chart to Build Number Sense provides teachers with engaging activities based on important mathematical ideas; clear and concise lessons structured with the "introduce, explore, summarize" format; questions and tips to guide, assess, and extend student thinking; and on-the-spot professional development in the form of Teacher Reflections and A Child's Mind. This resource is an important companion text to any math program!

> —*Karen Economopoulos, Codirector, Investigations in Number, Data and Space*

It Makes Sense! Using the Hundreds Chart to Build Number Sense is a superb resource for teachers! The content is rich, focused on the big ideas of mathematics, appropriate for young students, and conceptually based. The teaching methods are carefully detailed; it is obvious that these are lessons that have been taught to real children in real settings. Melissa and Stephanie have done a masterful job of describing what teaching for understanding really means.

> —*Juanita V. Copley, Professor Emerita, University of Houston*

I've used the activities in *It Makes Sense!* numerous times in my class. Having the visual of the hundreds chart is very helpful for my students. My students now have a grasp of sequencing, patterns, addition, subtraction, and the relationship between the numbers. Through repeated practice, they are able to internalize these skills, all while having fun playing a game.

> —*Shannon Sullivan, First Grade Team Leader/ESL Coordinator,*
> *Eickenroht Elementary, Houston, Texas*

It Makes Sense! Using the Hundreds Chart to Build Number Sense . . . and I couldn't agree more! In a primary math classroom, is there any other tool that is more important and appropriate than the hundreds chart? Melissa and Stephanie have teamed together again to provide teachers with engaging lessons accessible to all! Your students build, navigate, investigate, and communicate their way to a stronger sense of numbers. I am not sure if you can find many first graders who wouldn't love to build a wacky hundreds chart and then talk about it with their peers. What a fabulous resource for educators!

> —*Beth Terry, Math Specialist, Alexandria City Public Schools, Virginia,*
> *2004 PAEMST Awardee—Colorado*

This rich resource provides teachers with easy-to-implement lessons that help children use the hundreds chart to develop key base-ten number concepts. Not only does this book offer engaging activities that can be used with any textbook series, but it also comes with ideas for homework, technology connections, and tips for supporting language learners. *It Makes Sense!* is at the top of my list when recommending math resources that support number sense development.

> —*Rusty Bresser, Lecturer and Supervisor of Teacher Education at the*
> *University of California, San Diego and Coauthor of*
> Developing Number Sense, Grades 3–6

A Message from Heinemann

Heinemann's math professional resources are written by educators, for educators, to support student-centered teaching and learning. Our authors provide classroom-tested guidance, advice, and proven best practices to help teachers increase their comfort and confidence with teaching math. We believe a focus on reasoning and understanding is the pathway to helping students make sense of the mathematics they're learning.

This resource was originally published by Math Solutions, a company long dedicated to similar ideals and aims as Heinemann. In 2022, Math Solutions Publications became part of Heinemann. While the logo on the cover is different, the heart of Math Solutions lives in these pages: that teaching math well calls for increasing our understanding of the math we teach, seeking deeper insights into how students learn mathematics, and refining our lessons to best promote students' learning.

To learn more about our resources and authors, please visit Heinemann.com/Math.

Contents

Acknowledgments   *xiii*

How to Use This Resource   *xv*

SECTION I: Lessons Using the Hundreds Chart

L-1   Building the Hundreds Chart (Version 1)   6

L-2   Building the Hundreds Chart (Version 2)   12

L-3   Arrow Arithmetic   20

L-4   Building a Wacky Hundreds Chart   28

L-5   One More or One Less   37

L-6   Ten More or Ten Less   47

L-7   Hundreds Chart Riddles   58

L-8   Look, Quick!   66

L-9   Missing Number Puzzles   73

L-10 From Here to There: Solving
      Comparison Problems   80

SECTION II: Games Using the Hundreds Chart

G-1   Number Chart Bingo!   97

G-2   Too High, Too Low   103

G-3   Fill It Up!   111

G-4 Mystery Squares   117

G-5 Don't Get Lost   123

G-6 Hippety Hop   133

G-7 Race to 100   142

G-8 101 and Out!   150

G-9 The Larger Difference   161

G-10 How Far Away?   173

Reproducibles   *181*

Index   *239*

All reproducibles are available as downloadable, printable versions at http://hein.pub/MathOLR. Registration information and key code can be found on page xx in the frontmatter. Connections to standards are also available online. To access, follow the instructions for accessing the online reproducibles.

Reproducibles

In addition to being available in this resource, downloadable printable versions are available online. See page xx for detailed access and registration instructions.

1 Arrow Clue Cards   183

2 Spinners: One Less or One More and
   -1 or +1   186

3 Blank Counting Board: 1–20   187

4 Blank Counting Board: 1–30   188

5 Blank Counting Board: 1–50   189

6 Numbered Counting Board: 1–20   190

7 Numbered Counting Board: 1–30   191

8 Numbered Counting Board: 1–50   192

9 Teacher Checklist: One More or One Less   193

10 Teacher Checklist: Ten More or Ten Less   194

11 Hundreds Chart Riddles   195

12 Missing Number Puzzles   198

13 Missing Number Puzzles Assessment   202

14 From Here to There Word Problems   203

15 Number Chart Bingo! Cards   204

16 Fill It Up! Cards   210

17 Mystery Squares Masks   211

18 Race to 100: Fives Strips   215

19 Race to 100: Tens Strips   216

20 Race to 100: Action Cards   217

21 Race to 100: Question Cards   218

22 101 and Out! Recording Sheet   219

23   101 and Out! Assessment Sheet   220

24   The Larger Difference Recording Sheet   221

The following reproducibles are referenced and used throughout the book:

A   The Hundreds Chart (1–100)   222

B   The Fifty Chart (1–50)   223

C   101–200 Chart   224

D   10-by-10 Grid   225

E   10-by-5 Grid   226

G-1R   Number Chart Bingo! Game Directions   227

G-2R   Too High, Too Low Game Directions   228

G-3R   Fill It Up! Game Directions   229

G-4R   Mystery Squares Game Directions   230

G-5R   Don't Get Lost Game Directions   231

G-6Ra   Hippety Hop, Cooperative Group
Version Game Directions   232

G-6Rb   Hippety Hop, Competitive Version
Game Directions   233

G-7R   Race to 100 Game Directions   234

G-8R   101 and Out Game Directions   235

G-9R   The Larger Difference Game Directions   236

G-10R   How Far Away? Game Directions   237

All reproducibles are available as downloadable, printable versions at http://hein.pub/MathOLR. Registration information and key code can be found on page xx in the frontmatter.

Teacher Reflections

My *Building the Hundreds Chart* Experiences:
Determining Appropriate Levels   10

My Experiences Playing *Building
a Wacky Hundreds Chart*   34

My Experiences with
One More or One Less   43

My Experiences with
Ten More or Ten Less   55

My Experiences with
Hundreds Chart Riddles   64

My Experiences with
Missing Number Puzzles   77

My Experiences with *From Here to There*:
Scribing Students' Strategies   89

My Experiences with
Number Chart Bingo!   102

A Whole-Class Discussion on
Too High, Too Low   109

My Experiences with Summarizing
Don't Get Lost   129

My Experiences Preparing Students for the
Exploration Part of *Hippety Hop*   139

Recording Student Thinking:

    Class Discussions   149

My Experiences in Summarizing

    101 and Out!   157

My Experiences with Student

    Recordings for *The Larger Difference*   171

Assessments

One More or One Less   45

Ten More or Ten Less   56

Hundreds Chart Riddles   65

Acknowledgments

We have been extremely fortunate to learn from Marilyn Burns and would like to thank her for her commitment and passion for mathematics education.

We would like to thank the teachers who graciously allowed us to work with their students: Carol Havemann, Javier Domingez, Shannon Sullivan, and Sicely Williams at Eickenroht Elementary in Spring ISD in Houston, Texas; and Kami Burgin at Brandenburgh Elementary in Irving, Texas.

Thanks to Elizabeth Sweeney and Maryann Wickett for sharing the game *Hippety Hop* with us, and allowing us to include it in the book. Also to Amy Mayfield for the original idea for *Build a Wacky Hundreds Chart*. We are so lucky to work with such talented colleagues.

We'd like to thank Jamie Cross for her skillful guidance throughout this project. Her cheerful disposition kept us smiling through it all, and her insightful questions helped us make the book stronger. Thanks, too, to Denise Botelho for minding our Ps and Qs, bookwise.

—Melissa Conklin and Stephanie Sheffield

I'd like to thank Robbie Green, principal of Eickenroht Elementary for his friendship and support of my work and my writing. His leadership and vision create in our school an atmosphere where student thinking and reasoning are encouraged and valued. Thanks also to my friend and colleague Kelly Hamilton-McMahon for being my constant cheerleader and for her listening ear. Thanks to my whole family who were patient while I wrote, and who encouraged me to keep going. My work on this book is lovingly dedicated to my mentor and friend Katharine Kharas, who helped me be a better teacher and a better person.

—Stephanie Sheffield

I'd like to thank my husband, parents, and in-laws for caring for and loving on my daughter during the writing of this book. Their support and encouragement have been invaluable throughout this process.

—Melissa Conklin

How to Use This Resource

What is a hundreds chart?

A hundreds chart is a 10-by-10 grid with the numbers one to one hundred printed in the squares. A hundreds chart can be sized so that each student has her or his own hundreds chart, or it can be poster-size for use with the whole class. Some hundreds charts have clear pockets stitched onto vinyl or fabric to allow easy insertion and removal of number cards. We refer to these charts as *pocket hundreds charts* throughout this resource, and recommend the use of them; moveable numbers transform a hundreds chart into a highly engaging manipulative. A hundreds chart that can be photocopied is provided in this resource as Reproducible A.

A pocket hundreds chart filled with number cards 1 through 100.

1	2	3	4	5	6	7	8	9	10
11	12	13	14	15	16	17	18	19	20
21	22	23	24	25	26	27	28	29	30
31	32	33	34	35	36	37	38	39	40
41	42	43	44	45	46	47	48	49	50
51	52	53	54	55	56	57	58	59	60
61	62	63	64	65	66	67	68	69	70
71	72	73	74	75	76	77	78	79	80
81	82	83	84	85	86	87	88	89	90
91	92	93	94	95	96	97	98	99	100

A version of the hundreds chart for individual use (available as Reproducible A).

Why use a hundreds chart?

The purpose of a hundreds chart is to provide a framework for students to think about our base ten number system and to allow students to build a mental model of the mathematical structure of our number system. Hundreds charts allow children to explore concepts from counting to adding two-digit numbers.

It Makes Sense! Using the Hundreds Chart to Build Number Sense includes lessons that help students look for and make sense of the pattern and structure of the hundreds chart intentionally to become computationally flexible and fluent. The lessons in *It Makes Sense! Using the Hundreds Chart to Build Number Sense* transform a hundreds chart from a poster on the wall to an interactive tool used and internalized by the students.

The National Council of Teachers of Mathematics (or NCTM) document *Principles and Standards for School Mathematics* states, "In prekindergarten through grade 2 all students should use multiple models to develop initial understandings of place value and the base-ten number system." The hundreds chart is one such model—in fact, one of the most valuable ones.

Why these lessons?

The lessons and games we selected for *It Makes Sense! Using the Hundreds Chart to Build Number Sense* are student-tested favorites. We have taught them time and time again in our own classrooms and in the classrooms of other teachers who invite us to share model teaching with them. The lessons are designed intentionally to provide students with opportunities to think, reason, and communicate about numbers. Many of the lessons and games are intended to be revisited throughout the school year to give students repeated experiences in building number sense. Most of the lessons also build on each other, or provide alternate ways of approaching the same concept, giving students multiple ways to access mathematical knowledge.

In our classrooms, hundreds charts are always available to our students, whether in the form of a pocket chart, individual laminated copies placed in an easily accessible location, or paper copies glued inside each student's math journal. Our students add to their own repertoires of techniques and strategies as they became comfortable playing the games and thinking about the lessons they've encountered.

Unfortunately, many times when we visit other teachers' classrooms we see that, although there may be a hundreds pocket chart or a poster on the wall, teachers aren't exactly sure what to do with it. Frequently, we find that the only use of hundreds chart in classrooms is to keep track of the number of days students have been in school. This is such a disservice to the value of a hundreds chart, and we're here to help! Every lesson and game included in this resource supports teachers in making the most of the hundreds chart, helping their students develop strategies and build concepts needed for a robust understanding of numbers and place value.

Every lesson features user-friendly directions and appropriate, clear questions to help teachers check for understanding and extend their students' thinking. Communication about students' thinking plays a key role in the lessons. It is our hope that students return to the lessons and games again and again, each time gaining more facility with numerical reasoning, and improving their ability to communicate their understanding.

How do I use the lessons?

Two Categories

This resource is divided into two categories: lessons and games. The lessons feature activities that introduce students to the hundreds chart and its function as a tool for thinking about numbers, their magnitude, and their relationship to each other. The lessons also encourage the use of a hundreds chart as a framework for thinking about computation of one- and two-digit numbers. The games section offers games that help students develop numerical fluency, as well as challenge them to think strategically and play cooperatively.

Where to Start

In the "Related Lessons" section of each lesson and game, you'll get suggestions for what to teach next. When you first use the hundreds chart, we suggest starting with the lessons titled *Building the Hundreds Chart* (L-1 and L-2) and *Arrow Arithmetic* (L-3). All the other lessons use skills introduced in these lessons.

Lesson and Game Overview

Each lesson and game opens with an overview that gives you an opportunity to become acquainted with the mathematical goals of the lesson, as well as what students will be doing.

Time

The "Time" section of each lesson gives a general prediction of the time it will take to carry out the lesson. In general, each lesson takes thirty to forty minutes. Games usually take less time (ten to thirty minutes) to complete. Repetition is encouraged for many of the lessons and games.

Materials

The following is a basic list of materials needed for the lessons; each lesson and game opens with a specific list. When possible, reproducibles are provided for your convenience.

▶ a pocket hundreds chart with removable cards labeled *1* through *100* for whole-class use (cards can be created using Reproducible A)

▶ transparent markers for the pocket hundreds chart (These markers are available commercially through math catalogs, or can be made by cutting squares from a colored transparency the same size as the removable cards. As an alternative, you can cut squares of construction paper that are slightly larger than the removable cards to place behind the numbers to which you want to draw attention.)

▶ hundreds charts for individual student use (These can be printed on paper or cardstock using Reproducible A. Laminate the charts to help them last longer.)

▶ 20 counters for each student (For consistency, the term *counters* is used throughout this resource. There are a variety of options for counters: Snap Cubes, Unifix cubes, color tiles, or two-color counters. You may also consider using everyday objects such as lima beans, pennies, dimes, or small buttons. We recommend commercially available small, translucent discs, because students can still read the numbers under these counters when using the hundreds chart.)

> a projected hundreds chart (Some lessons require that the teacher use a projected hundreds chart, which can be a paper copy of a chart [Reproducible A] projected via a document camera or overhead projector. There are many hundreds charts available for use with interactive whiteboards as well. These can be found on the NCTM website [www.nctm.org] or through a quick Internet search.)

Key Questions

Each lesson offers key questions to promote student thinking, class discussions, and assessment of what students know. These carefully planned questions elicit deeper thinking and reasoning among students, and are meant to be asked throughout the lesson or game. Often, it is necessary to scribe or record student thinking. Recording student thinking connects a child's thinking to representations (such as pictures) or to symbols (such as numbers). It allows the student who is speaking, and others in the class, to observe their thinking visually.

Teaching Directions

The teaching directions are presented in a step-by-step lesson plan with references to when and how to use the key questions, and what a student might be thinking. Some of the lessons are divided into parts to make the planning process more manageable.

Additional Teaching Insights

In addition to what we have presented thus far, teaching insights are provided throughout the lessons in the following ways:

> "Math Matters!" sections provide an opportunity to deepen one's own math content.

> "Teaching Tip" and "Technology Tip" sections offer insights to help make the session run smoothly, including suggestions for using interactive whiteboards.

> "A Child's Mind . . ." sections give you an opportunity to read how or why your own students may think about a problem.

> "Differentiating Your Instruction" sections offer extensions or modifications to meet all learners' needs.

> "Time Saver" sections provide insights for saving time in lesson preparation.

> "Extend Their Learning!" sections are featured in some lessons to continue the learning of groups of students or the whole class.

> "Teacher Reflections" sections are included throughout the book to offer insight into experiences that have shaped our own thinking about teaching.

How to Access Online Resources

Follow these instructions to register and access downloadable reproducibles for *It Makes Sense! Using the Hundreds Chart to Build Number Sense*:

1. Go to http://hein.pub/MathOLR and click or tap the Create New Account button at the bottom of the Log In form.
2. Create an account. You will receive a confirmation email when your account has been created.
3. Once your account has been created, you will be taken to the Product Registration page. Click Register on the product you would like to access (in this case, *It Makes Sense! Using the Hundreds Chart to Build Number Sense*).

Key Code: IMSHC

4. Enter key code **IMSHC** and click or tap the Submit Key Code button.
5. Click or tap the Complete Registration button.
6. To access online resources at any time, visit your account page.

Connections to Standards

Tables are available online to help you connect the provided games and lessons with standards. Using the tables alongside your own curriculum, standards, or pacing guides will help you determine which lessons meet the concepts and skills you are in need of addressing with your students. To access the tables, follow the instructions above for accessing the downloadable reproducibles.

More Resources in the Series!

We are excited to share this resource, *It Makes Sense! Using the Hundreds Chart to Build Number Sense*, as one of several resources in the It Makes Sense! series. For more titles, see Heinemann.com/Math.

It Makes Sense!

Using the Hundreds Chart to Build Number Sense

Grades K–2

Lessons Using the Hundreds Chart

L-1   Building the Hundreds Chart (Version 1)   6

L-2   Building the Hundreds Chart (Version 2)   12

L-3   Arrow Arithmetic   20

L-4   Building a Wacky Hundreds Chart   28

L-5   One More or One Less   37

L-6   Ten More or Ten Less   47

L-7   Hundreds Chart Riddles   58

L-8   Look, Quick!   66

L-9   Missing Number Puzzles   73

L-10   From Here to There: Solving Comparison Problems   80

Why these lessons?

The lessons in this section are designed to introduce students to the hundreds chart as a tool for understanding our number system more completely, as well as to help students create a mental image of the hundreds chart that they can use in subsequent lessons. Learning to use a hundreds chart as a tool for adding and subtracting is one of the goals of this resource, along with improving their understanding of our base ten number system. Some of the lessons are structured to follow a lesson plan format divided into three parts: an introduction, an exploration, and a summary.

Three Parts of a Lesson

1. Introduce

2. Explore

3. Summarize

Introduce

The purpose of the introduction is to familiarize students with the problem and to connect with students' prior knowledge. This may mean solving a less complicated problem or beginning to solve the problem on which students will work during the exploration stage. The introduction is also the stage to present vocabulary that may be used in the student exploration part of the lesson.

Explore

During the exploration phase, students are involved in the main work of the problem. The purpose of this stage is to give students opportunities to discover, deepen, and extend their understanding of numbers and place value.

Summarize

Last, the purpose of the summary is to cement students' learning and allow them to communicate their thinking about the problem. This section of the lesson allows students to share their strategies and to hear other students share strategies they might not have tried.

How much time do these lessons require?

Lessons in this section may take more than one class period. During the initial lesson, consider introducing the problem and giving students time to explore the problem (thus working through the introduction and exploration stages). Begin the summary during the next math period. Saving the summary for a later math period, rather than working through all three stages in one period, gives students time to think about their exploration. In addition, students tend to become less restless and can talk longer about what they have learned when the summary takes place at the beginning of a period rather than at the end.

Some explorations may take two full math periods. At the end of the first day, facilitate a class discussion as a kind of check-in with students. Ask questions to help them think over what they have been exploring: What do they understand? What solutions have they found? What difficulties are they encountering? This discussion provides support for all students when they come back to complete the lesson activity on the second day. At the end of the second day, check in again with another class discussion. Have any new insights or discoveries been made?

If there are students who need five or ten minutes more than what has been allotted to complete exploration, reserve time for those students to work on the activity before you begin the summary.

Teaching Tip

Check-in Questions for Use at the End of the Exploration Stage of a Lesson

▶ What do you understand?

▶ What solutions did you find?

▶ What difficulties are you having?

▶ What new insights or discoveries did you make?

What is my role as teacher in these lessons?

At every stage of the lesson, your role is an active one. During the lesson introduction, give directions clearly and concisely. We want students to understand the activity without giving away the answer.

As students work through the lesson, use the key questions (included in the "Key Questions" section in each lesson) to probe students' thinking and to extend their understanding. When students are struggling with a concept, work with them by asking questions and referring back to the introduction. Refrain from telling them the answer.

At the end of the lesson, facilitate a discussion on the mathematical goals of the lesson. This discussion might include introducing or revisiting key vocabulary, looking for patterns, and making generalizations. To begin the summary, you might find it helpful to allow students to talk to their partners before beginning a whole-class discussion. What discoveries did they make during the lesson? What did they learn during their explorations? Starting with partner talk allows students to feel the value of being listened to while practicing what they may say during the whole-class discussion.

After partner talk, call on a few students to share their thinking or their work. (Note that the goal is not to call on every student to come to the front of the room to share his or her thinking, simply because of the amount of time involved to complete this activity.) As students share their thoughts, record their thinking where everyone can see it. This helps students make connections between mathematical thinking and symbolic representation. In the primary grades, this visible record is especially important. Repeated opportunities to see the symbolic representations eventually help students begin to use representations on their own.

Lesson 1 Building the Hundreds Chart (Version 1)

Overview

In this lesson, students build a hundreds chart one number at a time. The lesson serves as an initial introduction to the hundreds chart. Whether this lesson is taught during the first weeks of school, in the middle of the year, or even later, it serves as a formative assessment of students' ability to read numbers, as well as an assessment of their understanding of *before* and *after*.

Related Lessons

Consider these lessons as a follow-up (in this order):

▶ L-3 Arrow Arithmetic

▶ L-2 Building the Hundreds Chart (Version 2)

Key Questions

▶ Where does this number belong on the hundreds chart?

▶ How did you know the number fits there?

Time

15 to 20 minutes, three to five times during the course of a week, repeated several times during the year

Materials

pocket hundreds chart with removable number cards *or*

hundreds chart projected on screen or interactive whiteboard

Teaching Directions

1. Before beginning this lesson, prepare a pocket hundreds chart by placing these number cards in the pockets: 4, 10, 17, 32, and 48. Hold the rest of the numbers in your hands, arranged in order so that you can choose a number easily.

2. Gather students together so they can see the pocket hundreds chart or the projected hundreds chart easily.

3. Hold up the first card to be placed: 18. Ask, "Who would like to come up and place this number card where it belongs on the hundreds chart?"

(continued)

Differentiating Your Instruction

Making Decisions Before You Begin
Before beginning this lesson, think about your students and their previous experiences with the hundreds chart. Kindergarten teachers may initially want to use only the numbers one through fifty, but plan to repeat the lesson later in the year with all the numbers. First-grade teachers need to decide whether to try to build an entire hundreds chart or a smaller subchart at the beginning of the year. Even if you plan to build the whole chart during the course of a week, you might want to consider starting the first day with numbers from one through fifty.

Teaching Tip

Choosing Numbers
As you call students forward to place numbers in the chart, choose numbers based on what you know or want to know about your students' number knowledge. For instance, if you are concerned about whether a student can count on successfully, you might offer him a number that is two or three numbers more than a number that is already placed, giving him the opportunity to use that skill if he chooses.

Technology Tip

Using an Interactive Whiteboard
If you are using an interactive whiteboard, project an interactive hundreds chart and turn over all the numbers except 4, 10, 17, 32, and 48. If you do not have access to an interactive hundreds chart, use a 10-by-10 grid and the interactive pen to record the numbers. For Step 3, call out the number eighteen and ask, "Who knows where eighteen belongs and would like to come touch the spot so that the number turns over?" If you are using an interactive whiteboard with a 10-by-10 grid, call out the number eighteen and ask, "Who knows where eighteen belongs and would like to come record it in the correct place?"

Teaching Tip

Reading Two-Digit Numbers

If a student reads the number incorrectly, tell the student the correct way to read the number while you move your finger under the number, but don't stop at this time and try to explain the place-value concept behind why the number is written as it is. Make a note of which students are having difficulty reading two-digit numbers so that you can provide additional experiences to strengthen this skill at a later time.

Technology Tip

Using an Interactive Whiteboard

If you are using an interactive whiteboard, students do not have the opportunity to read numbers from the cards (rather than cards, you simply call out the numbers). Thus, it may be advantageous to use the pocket hundreds chart for this first lesson, or switch up between the two displays (interactive whiteboard and pocket chart) in repeated use of the lesson.

4. Call on a volunteer. Before giving the card to her, ask her to read the number. If she reads it incorrectly—as eighty-one, for instance— say, "This number is eighteen. Can you find the place where it fits on the chart?" If the student answers correctly the first time, allow her to place the card, then ask, "Tell us how you knew the card fit there." Students will probably respond that they know that the number eighteen comes after the number seventeen, although some will have to start at number one and count the spaces until they get to eighteen.

5. Continue calling on students to come forward and place numbers into the hundreds chart. Each time you do this, ask the student to explain how she knows the number fits where she has placed it. All students will benefit every time they have the opportunity to explain their thinking, or have to listen to their classmates explain theirs.

A Child's Mind . . .

When to End the Lesson

Watch your class carefully for signs of restlessness and fatigue. Because this lesson is intended for the beginning of the year, students will have limited ability to sit still while just one student at a time participates. When students become squirmy, move to a different activity, then return to this one later. This lesson can be broken down easily into several sessions with no loss of continuity.

Extend Their Learning!

After building an entire hundreds chart, add the activity to choices for math stations. During independent work time, students may choose to rebuild the hundreds chart alone or with a partner. Students enjoy doing this again and again, and even make a game of how quickly they can rebuild the chart.

Time Saver

When students come into class in the morning, ask the first one or two who get finished with their morning jobs to remove all the cards from the pocket hundreds chart and mix up the cards so the cards are ready for the extension activity during math time.

Teacher Reflection

My *Building the Hundreds Chart* Experiences: Determining Appropriate Levels

Building the Hundreds Chart is an activity appropriate for kindergarten and first or second grades. There are several decisions I make so that the lesson is appropriate for children at each level.

Kindergarten

Many kindergartners are still working on the oral counting sequence to one hundred. They may also be learning to connect the numbers they say with the numerals they represent. For these reasons, building a chart all the way to one hundred may not be appropriate at the beginning of the year. I gauge my students' needs and abilities as I set up the lesson. I may choose to begin with only the numbers one through thirty, then as the year progresses and I become more confident in my students' number knowledge, I repeat the lesson, first with the numbers one through fifty, and finally with all the numbers on the hundreds chart. In this way, I keep the experience within the grasp of my students, but always give them a challenge to work toward.

FIGURE L-1.1 Mrs. Conklin holds up number card 13 and pauses to give first graders an opportunity to think about where it should be placed.

First Grade

At the beginning of the year, when I initiate this lesson with first graders, I often use only the numbers one through fifty. I want to present a lesson that is not overwhelming to my students, as a nearly blank hundreds chart may be. I also want to start with lessons that can be completed within a week; near the beginning of the year, I am still unsure of the abilities of all my students. After I assess their understanding of basic number concepts, as well as their counting skills, I am better able to determine which students are ready for the challenge of the whole chart, and which students still need a modified chart with which to work. This knowledge helps me as I choose numbers to offer each child to place on the chart.

Second Grade

Although I would love for every one of my second graders to enter my class with a solid familiarity of the hundreds chart, it doesn't always happen. Once again, at the beginning of the year, I am careful not to overwhelm my students. As we begin to complete the first half of the hundreds chart, I get a sense of how quickly my students can place numbers and how well they can explain how they know where numbers fit. I keep the following questions in mind during these early days.

Questions to Help Determine Students' Number Sense

▶ Do students have an understanding that moving up and down the hundreds chart involves adding and subtracting ten?

▶ When handed a number card, can students find the general location of the card quickly? For example, if handed the number card 89, do they immediately look toward the bottom of the hundreds chart?

▶ Do students count from one for a number like twenty-three, or do they look for a larger number already placed on the hundreds chart from which to count on?

▶ Can students read two-digit numbers correctly or do they sometimes reverse the digits?

FIGURE L-1.2 Victor counts on from number card 10 before placing 13 in the correct spot on a hundreds chart.

I know that multiple experiences with the hundreds chart benefit students who are still constructing their understanding of the number system. Some second graders benefit from rebuilding the chart repeatedly throughout the year. I keep this in mind and make sure to include this as an option during independent practice time.

Lesson 2 Building the Hundreds Chart (Version 2)

Overview

In this lesson, students use number relations and mental math to rebuild the hundreds chart. Whenever they place a number on the chart, they must explain their reasoning for doing so by using one of four sentence frames (provided with the lesson). This lesson helps students develop computational fluency with adding and subtracting one and ten from numbers on the hundreds chart.

Related Lessons

You might teach the following lesson first:

▶ L-3 Arrow Arithmetic

Consider this lesson as a follow-up:

▶ L-6 Ten More or Ten Less

Key Questions

▶ How did you know to play that number card?

▶ What number card is the player holding?

Time

20 minutes

Materials

pocket hundreds chart with removable number cards *or*

hundreds chart projected on screen or interactive whiteboard

The Hundreds Chart (1–100) (Reproducible A), numbers cut apart into cards (if using an interactive whiteboard)

sentence frames (see "Teaching Directions")

optional: colored blank cards that fit in pocket hundreds chart

Teaching Directions

1. Before students enter the classroom, remove all number cards from the hundreds chart except for card 36 (also hold on to card 46 because it will be used as a model later in the lesson).

2. Gather students together so they can easily see the pocket hundreds chart or the projected hundreds chart.

3. Tell students that the focus of the lesson is to rebuild the hundreds chart. Each student will receive a few number cards from the hundreds chart. To place a number on the hundreds chart, the number must fit below, above, to the left, or to the right of a number that has already been placed. Ask students to think about describing, in mathematical terms, what it means to move up, down, left, and right on a hundreds chart. Tell students to turn and talk about this with a partner.

4. Call on a few students to explain, in mathematical terms, what it means to move up, down, left, and right.

   Examples of Student Thinking

   "Add one."

   "Increase by ten."

   "Subtract one."

   "Get smaller by ten."

5. Introduce the following sentence frames to students:

Technology Tip

Using an Interactive Whiteboard
If you are using an interactive whiteboard, make a copy of The Hundreds Chart (Reproducible A), cut apart the numbers, and place all number cards except 36 and 46 in a bag. Also, project a 10-by-10 grid and write the number *36* (using an interactive pen) in the appropriate square. Explain that students will use the interactive pen to write the number on the whiteboard and then give you their number card.

Structure for Writing Riddles

Sentence Frames
▶ My number is one more than ___ [number].
▶ My number is one less than ___ [number].
▶ My number is ten more than ___ [number].
▶ My number is ten less than ___ [number].

Tell students they should use the frames when explaining their placement of the number they have in the hundreds chart.

Teaching Tip

Visual Support

For additional support, point to the number 36, then ask the question using the first sentence frame, "What number is one more?" Point to the empty place where 37 belongs. Continue this visual support for the remaining three sentence frames (for additional insights as to why this is done, see "Math Matters! The Importance of Touching the Numbers" on page 18 in this lesson).

6. Ask students to think about what four numbers could be played on the chart right now. Ask students to turn and talk to a partner before you call on volunteers to share their thoughts.

7. Hold up the number 46 and use the sentence frame to model for students. "My number is ten more than thirty-six." Place card 46 in the hundreds chart. Tell students that now they may play off the numbers 36 or 46. To clarify any confusion students may have, ask them to think about what numbers can now be played. Tell them to turn and talk to a partner, then call on volunteers to share their thoughts. Numbers that can be played, according to the sentence frames, are 26, 35, 37, 45, 47, and 56. For more clarification, place colored blank squares in all the spaces that are now open for play. Remove the colored squares after your explanation.

FIGURE L-2.1 Mrs. Conklin reminds students how to use the sentence frames when placing the numbers on a hundreds chart.

8. Mix up the number cards and pass them out to students until all the cards are gone. Tell students they will each get a turn to place numbers on the hundreds chart. If they have more than one number ca rd that is playable, they are welcome to put more than one number card in the hundreds chart.

Technology Tip

Using an Interactive Whiteboard
If an interactive whiteboard is being used, remind students that they will record the number that is written on one of their number cards on the interactive whiteboard (using the interactive pen) and will then hand you their number card.

A Child's Mind . . .

Competition?
Tell students this is not a competitive game. The object is to build the chart, not to be the first person to get rid of the number cards they are holding.

FIGURE L-2.2 First grader Diego explains where the number 70 goes using the sentence frame, "My number is ten more than sixty."

Teaching Tip

Who Goes First?

If students are sitting in a whole-group area, have students in the first row go first, followed by those in the second row, and so on. Or have students sit in a semicircle around the hundreds chart and start at one end and move to the next student. If students are sitting at tables, have students sitting at one table go first, followed by the next table and so on.

A Child's Mind . . .

Getting Help from Others

Tell students they are welcome to ask their peers for help, but they may not tell their peers what cards to play unless asked.

9. Have students come up, one by one, and play their number cards. Make sure they use the sentence frames to voice their thinking out loud. Stop periodically and review which number cards are playable. Encourage students to check their number cards to determine whether they have playable cards.

10. The activity ends when all cards have been played.

FIGURE L-2.3 JP uses the sentence frame "My number is less than forty" to explain where the number 39 belongs.

Extend Their Learning!

After students have played several times and are comfortable using the sentence frames, introduce the extension presented here. Its purpose is to give students the opportunity to do mental math. Tell students that when their peer says the sentence frame, they must call out what number the person is holding *before* it is placed in the hundreds chart. Model an example by placing the number 36 as the starting number and say, "My number is one more than thirty-six." Give students a few seconds to think, then ask them to call out the number that is one more than thirty-six. After students say "Thirty-seven!" place the number card 37 in the hundreds chart.

Pass out the number cards and begin to play the game as you usually do. For every couple of students who come up to place a number card, ask them to do the extension. In other words, tell them to say the sentence frame, then ask the other students to call out the number they think the student is holding *before* the student places his card in the chart.

A Child's Mind . . .

Providing Time to Think
For all students to have time to think before hearing the answer, give a cue—such as counting "One, two, three"—before allowing students to call out the number.

Modification: Play Without Sentence Frames

Do the activity several times *without* the sentence frames. Tell students they may play numbers cards that are below, above, to the left, or to the right of the numbers that have already been played. The purpose for this modification is to allow students an opportunity to become familiar with the structure of the hundreds chart before attaching ideas about computation.

Modification: Kindergarten

Modify the steps as follows to make this lesson most appropriate for kindergarteners:

1. Remove all the number cards from the hundreds chart and place cards 31 to 100 to the side. Place a few numbers in the hundreds chart, such as 4, 17, 21, and 27.

2. Explain to the students they will work to build the chart from one to thirty by placing numbers that are *next to* the numbers already in the hundreds chart.

3. Point to the number 4 and move one space to where the number 5 will go. Ask the students, "How many moves did I make?" When they say "one," acknowledge that you are adding one. Again, point to the number 4 and move one space to where the number 3 will go. Ask the students, "How many moves did I make?" When they say "one," acknowledge that three is one less than four. Ask students, "What number is one more than four and what number is one less than four?" Repeat this process for the remaining numbers that are visible on the hundreds chart.

4. Tell students they will receive a number card and, when it is their turn, they may place the card in the hundreds chart if it is *one more* or *one less* than a card that has been played. Restate this another way by saying, "You may place your card in the hundreds chart if it is *before* or *after* a number card that has already been played."

5. Model holding up the number 16 and saying, "Sixteen is one less that seventeen" or "Sixteen comes before seventeen." Pass out a number card to each student. If you have left-over cards, keep those and play them when appropriate.

Math Matters!

The Importance of Touching the Numbers
Just as it is important to model for students how to touch each word when they are learning to read, it is also important to model touching a number on a hundreds chart and moving your finger forward or backward to show one more or one less than a number, respectively. In reading, children start out touching each word as they read it, and later begin to move their finger fluidly under a line of text as they read more fluently. So, too, in math do children begin by touching each number, one at a time, as they add or subtract on a hundreds chart. As their thinking develops, they become more comfortable making "jumps" on the chart, and showing those jumps with a more fluid movement of their finger.

6. Determine the order in which the students should play. When students play their number card, ask them to describe how they knew to play that card.

    Examples of Student Thinking

    "It's one more than ___."

    "It's before ___."

    "It's next to ___."

    Accept student thinking and rephrase it using *one more than* and *one less than* terms.

7. On subsequent days, repeat this game, playing with different ranges of numbers, such as twenty-five to fifty or thirty to sixty, for example.

FIGURE L-2.4 Mrs. Conklin plays *Building a Hundreds Chart* (*Version 2*) with a student.

Lesson 3

Arrow Arithmetic

Time

20 to 30 minutes to introduce the lesson

20 minutes for students to practice in pairs

10 to 15 minutes for whole-class discussion

Materials

pocket hundreds chart with removable number cards *or*

hundreds chart projected on screen or interactive whiteboard

individual whiteboards and markers *or*

student notebooks and pencils, one for each student

one copy of The Hundreds Chart (Reproducible A) for every pair of students

Extension

optional: Reproducible 1: Arrow Clue Cards, Sets A–C

Overview

This lesson builds on children's growing knowledge of the hundreds chart. Using arrows as clues, students solve puzzles on the chart. Each arrow corresponds to a movement on a hundreds chart: to the right, to the left, up, or down. The movements require students to add one or ten and to subtract one or ten. As students move around the hundreds chart visually, they continue to internalize the structure of the chart, which helps them as they use the chart to add and subtract two-digit numbers. This lesson is most appropriate for first and second graders.

Related Lessons

You might teach the following lessons first:

▶ L-1 Building the Hundreds Chart (Version 1)
▶ L-2 Building the Hundreds Chart (Version 2)

Consider this lesson as a follow-up:

▶ L-4 Building a Wacky Hundreds Chart

Key Questions

▶ What do you think this means?
▶ What does an up or down arrow mean when you are using it on a hundreds chart?
▶ What does a right or left arrow mean you are using it on a hundreds chart?
▶ What happens if you use an up arrow and a down arrow in the same clue?

Teaching Directions

Part 1: Introduce

1. Gather students together so they can see the hundreds chart easily.

2. Tell students, "I will be asking you to find a number that I have in mind. You will get two clues. One will be a starting number and one will be an arrow."

3. Ask students, "What do you know about arrows? Where might you see arrows?"

> **Possible Student Responses**
>
> "You shoot them with a bow."
>
> "You can see them on signs outside, like if a road curves."
>
> "Sometimes they are in books."
>
> "They tell you which way to go."

4. Explain that one meaning of the word *arrow* is a tool people use with bows to hunt or for sport. Another meaning of *arrow* is a symbol used to show direction. Ask a student to come to the board and draw an arrow. Point out that arrows have a pointed end that shows direction.

5. Tell students you are now going to give them an arrow clue. Write *25* → where everyone can see it. Ask students, "What do you think this means?"

> **Examples of Student Thinking**
>
> "It means you go over one space to the next number."
>
> "I think it means you have to move over to the right, so you land on twenty-six."
>
> "One arrow means one space."

Teaching Tip

Reviewing Vocabulary
Rather than assume that children know the meaning of words used in math, take a minute or two to be sure that everyone has a common understanding of the vocabulary you'll be using in a lesson.

6. After you've solicited several explanations, add = 26 to the end of the arrow clue, so it reads:

$$25 \rightarrow = 26$$

7. Suggest that students try to find the number—with their eyes—on the class hundreds chart, then look in the direction the arrow is pointing. Repeat Steps 5 through 7 for

$$25 \leftarrow = 24$$

$$25 \uparrow = 15$$

$$25 \downarrow = 35$$

8. Spend a few minutes writing other arrow clues and having students solve them and explain their thinking. Try

$$61 \rightarrow = ?$$

$$98 \uparrow = ?$$

$$39 \leftarrow = ?$$

9. After students are comfortable moving one space with an arrow clue, try giving them more than one arrow on a clue. For example, $47 \rightarrow \rightarrow = ?$ Ask students, "How did you know you should end on forty-nine?" Ask one student to explain his thinking.

Example of Student Thinking

"You start on forty-seven and you move over one space for every arrow, so that gets you to forty-nine."

Other arrow clues to try include the following:

$$27 \uparrow \uparrow = ? \text{ (Answer: 7)}$$

$$59 \leftarrow \leftarrow = ? \text{ (Answer: 57)}$$

$$34 \downarrow \downarrow = ? \text{ (Answer: 54)}$$

Differentiating Your Instruction

Arrow Clue Practice with a Partner

After you've presented several arrow clues to your students, if some of them are struggling to find the answer to the arrow clues quickly, consider stopping and having pairs of students practice giving each other clues. Give students individual whiteboards. Tell them to take turns writing a number on their whiteboard and drawing an arrow next to it. Then inform them that their partner should use the hundreds chart to find the number and move in the direction the arrow points. Tell students they should trade jobs with their partner after the first agrees that the correct number has been named.

Next try a few with mixed directions:

38 ← ↑ = ? (Answer: 27)

99 ↑ → = ? (Answer: 90)

72 ↓ ← = ? (Answer: 81)

46 ← ↑ = ? (Answer: 35)

Part 2: Explore

10. Now it's the students' turn to play! Pass out whiteboards and markers (or have students use a notebook and pencil) and allow them to practice with a partner. Review the directions with the class before they begin.

Playing Directions

a. Take turns writing an arrow clue for your partner.

b. Use one or two arrows in your clue.

c. Ask your partner to find the answer by moving her eyes from one number to another, following the direction of the arrows.

d. Talk to your partner. Ask, "How did you get the answer?"

A Child's Mind . . .

As the clues become more complex, students must look at the chart, find the starting place, make the initial move visually, then remember that number while they check for the direction of the second arrow. Then, they must make that move visually and mentally. Some children will use their fingers or hands to point at the hundreds chart at the front of the group as they do this. It's a harder task than it looks!

FIGURE L-3.1 Sofia writes an arrow clue, starting with the number 33, for her partner.

FIGURE L-3.2 Davion uses the hundreds chart to solve his partner Sofia's arrow clues.

A Child's Mind . . .

Touching the Hundreds Chart

When reading, children start out by touching each word as they read it. Later, they begin to move their finger fluidly under a line of text as they read more fluently. So, too, in math, do children begin by touching each number, one at a time, as they add or subtract on a hundreds chart. As their thinking develops, they become more comfortable making "jumps" on the chart and by showing those jumps with a more fluid movement of their fingers.

11. Circulate and observe students as they practice. Notice which students are able to locate the numbers visually and which use their fingers to point and move on a hundreds chart. Watch for students who can follow the clues confidently, and for those who are hesitant with their answers.

12. For those partners who seem to be solving the clues confidently, suggest that they add an arrow to the clue set. Tell them that it can either be a repeat of an arrow that they have already used (for example, $34 \rightarrow \downarrow = ?$ might

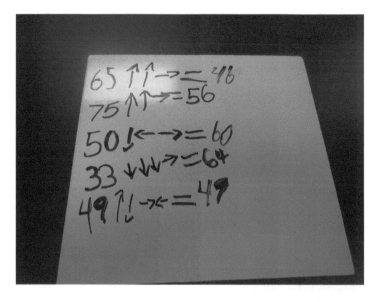

FIGURE L-3.3 Davion's arrow clues. He thought he was being tricky with his last clue by recording clues that cancel each other!

become $34 \rightarrow \downarrow \downarrow = ?$), or they could add a completely different arrow (for example, $34 \rightarrow \downarrow = ?$ might become $34 \uparrow \rightarrow \downarrow = ?$).

Part 3: Summarize

13. Gather students back together in front of the class hundreds chart used in the classroom.

14. Begin a discussion about what the students have just experienced; use the key questions listed at the beginning of this lesson. Ask students, "What happens to a number when the arrow points to the right?"

    Examples of Student Thinking

    "The numbers get bigger when you move that way."

    "It's like adding one."

    "Every box is one more than the one before."

15. Draw attention to the response, "It's like adding one." If no student suggests the connection to addition, suggest it yourself. Write $53 \rightarrow = ?$ Under this, write $53 + 1 = ?$

16. Next, write $76 \leftarrow = ?$ Ask for a volunteer to write this as a number sentence. First ask, "Are we adding or subtracting when we use a left arrow?" The student should record, $76 - 1 = 75$.

17. Continue the discussion by having more student volunteers record what the arrow clues mean using number sentences. Try the following:

    $92 \uparrow \uparrow = ?$ becomes $92 - 10 - 10 = ?$

    $40 \leftarrow \leftarrow \uparrow = ?$ becomes $40 - 1 - 1 - 10 = ?$

    $59 \downarrow \rightarrow \downarrow = ?$ becomes $59 + 10 + 1 + 10 = ?$

    $16 \rightarrow \uparrow \downarrow = ?$ becomes $16 + 1 - 10 + 10 = ?$

Teaching Tip

Continued Use of the Lesson
Look for opportunities to repeat this lesson or parts of this lesson throughout the school year. With practice, students become efficient with moving on a hundreds chart and connecting the movements to mathematical operations.

18. Ask, "What happens, as in the last example, when you have opposite arrows in the same clue?"

Examples of Student Thinking

"I think they undo each other. I think you're back on the number where you started."

"It's a plus and a minus, like you add ten, then you take away ten, so you really don't do anything at all."

"Your finger doesn't have to move, unless you have more up arrows than down arrows."

Extend Their Learning!

Diagonal Arrows

For students who need an extension, try presenting the following arrows: ↘↙ Encourage students to work together to figure out what all four of these arrows mean, and then write arrow clues.

Math Stations

Use Reproducible 1, Arrow Clue Cards: Sets A–C, to give students additional practice with arrow clues. Copy and cut out the clues provided (Set A contains the simplest clues, Set B is a bit more difficult, and Set C clues are challenging) or create your own cards. Place the clue cards in resealable bags, and have them available for students to use when there is extra time in class or during independent work time.

Lesson 4

Building a Wacky Hundreds Chart

Overview

In this cooperative lesson, which is a wacky twist on Lesson 1, *Building the Hundreds Chart (Version 1)*, students place numbers that are ten more or ten less (or one more or one less) than numbers that are already played. The lesson is played on the floor so that students are not constrained by the 10-by-10 dimensions of a pocket hundreds chart (part of the wackiness is that there are more options for where numbers can be placed!). Students focus on adding and subtracting one and ten without the visual clues of columns and rows.

Related Lessons

You might teach the following lessons first:

▶ L-1 Building the Hundreds Chart (Version 1)
▶ L-2 Building the Hundreds Chart (Version 2)

Consider these lessons as a follow-up:

▶ L-3 Arrow Arithmetic
▶ L-9 Missing Number Puzzles

Key Questions

▶ How is our wacky hundreds chart different from the one that usually hangs on the wall (or is on the interactive whiteboard, projector, and so forth)?

▶ How is it like the one that hangs on the wall (or is on the interactive whiteboard, projector, and so forth)?

▶ What choices did you have when playing this game that you did not have when placing the numbers in the pocket chart?

Time

25 to 35 minutes

Materials

number cards only from a pocket hundreds chart

Teaching Directions

Part 1: Introduce

1. Ask students to sit in a semicircle so they are all facing a large, clear space on the floor.

2. Mix up the hundreds chart number cards. Hold back one number card (a number that lands somewhere in the middle of the numbers being used, which allows students to place cards on all sides of that number right away). Of the remaining cards, give each student two cards.

3. Explain to students that they will be placing on the floor all the number cards that are usually in the pocket hundreds chart, and that their completed hundreds chart might be a bit wacky and probably won't look much like the one they are used to seeing. Remind them of the lesson, L-2 *Building the Hundreds Chart* (*Version 2*), when they used sentence frames to explain where they put missing numbers. Explain that during this activity, they will place numbers using the same rules: numbers that are one more or less or ten more or less than a number already placed.

4. Have students place their numbers face up on the floor in front of them. Ask them to read their numbers out loud to familiarize themselves with what they are working with.

Technology Tip

How Many Cards?

If you are introducing this lesson to your class for the first time, it's best to use only a portion of the hundreds chart numbers. Use twice as many numbers as you have students, plus one more. For example, if you have twenty-three students, use number cards 1 through 47. If you are playing this with kindergartners, use only the number cards 1 through 50.

FIGURE L-4.1 Students in Mr. Dominguez's class read the number cards they've been given to build a wacky hundreds chart.

5. Place the starter number card (the one you held back) in the middle of the open space.

Part 2: Explore

6. Explain that students will take turns placing the cards they are holding. For example, if you begin with card number 45, point to the first student in the group and ask, "Do you have a number card that is one more or one less than forty-five, or ten more or ten less?" If the first student does not have a card she can play, she must say, "Pass." In the beginning of the game, several students may have to pass before a student has one of the four cards that can be played; however, the game picks up speed as more cards are played. During each turn, a student may play only one card, even if they are holding more than one card that would fit on the chart.

7. After several turns, ask students to turn to a partner and tell him which cards could be played. For example, the arrangement of the cards on the floor might be

35

44 45 46 47

57

Number cards that can be played in this arrangement are 25, 34, 36, 43, 48, 54, 55, 56, 58, and 67. Encourage students to share how they know which numbers can be played next.

FIGURE L-4.2 Naomi places card 84 on the wacky hundreds chart. She explained, "Eighty-four is ten more than seventy-four."

8. The first time a multiple of ten is played, stop and highlight the choices students have next. Remind students that because this hundreds chart does not have a frame, numbers can be played anywhere they fit. For example, if card 50 is on the board, card 51 can go next to it on the right. It doesn't have to be moved down to the next row. In some cases there will be more than one correct placement for a card. For example:

```
23  24  25  26  27  28  29  30  31  32
        35  36  37
        45  46  47
            56  57
```

If the next student has card 33, she may choose to put it under card 23 or to the right of card 32.

Teaching Tip

Cooperative Class Games
This game is designed to be played cooperatively, so students are welcome to ask each other for help in deciding whether one of their cards can be placed on the board. However, students should not give help unless they are asked.

FIGURE L-4.3 Mr. Dominguez helps Jasmine, who speaks English as a second language, decide which card to add to the wacky hundreds chart.

Teaching Tip

Continued Use of the Lesson
This game can be played many times, and moves faster after students have played the first couple of times. Each time they play, students have the opportunity to think about where the numbers they have fit from one to one hundred.

9. When all the cards have been played, it's fun to take a photo of the final shape of the board and compare it with the final boards of other games.

Part 3: Summarize

10. Use the key questions presented at the beginning of this lesson to facilitate a class discussion about the wacky hundreds chart.

Modification

A Simpler Version for Kindergarten or First Grade

Some classes benefit from playing a modified version of *Building a Wacky Hundreds Chart* before playing the original version. For the modified version, pass out all the cards you plan to use and hold one back to be the starter card, as you would in the original game. However, rather than moving around the circle, giving each student an opportunity to play or pass, simply ask, "Who has a number that is one more or one less than the number on the floor?" Direct students to look through their number cards and raise their hand if they think they have a number to play. After a second card is placed, tell students to look to see whether they have a card that is one more or one less than either of the numbers on the floor. (Note: There are still only two numbers that can be played, but now students must find a number that is one less than the first number on the floor and one more than the second card.)

After the first few cards have been placed, or when you feel comfortable that your students understand what to do, add the next step by asking, "Who has a number that is either one more or one less than one of the numbers on the floor, or that is ten more or ten less than one of those numbers?" Allow students to check their cards and raise their hand when they think they have a number to play. Continue in this way, asking students to find cards that are one more or less or ten more or less than the numbers that have already been played. This modified version allows students more time to identify where their numbers can be played, rather than waiting for their turn.

Teacher Reflection

My Experiences Playing *Building a Wacky Hundreds Chart*

In gathering students for this lesson, I helped them rearrange themselves so that everyone had a view of the open space on the floor as well as some space directly in front of them for placing their cards. Each of my twenty-three students had two cards, and I chose card 23 to start the game. I then placed card 23 in the middle of the open space and explained, "When it's your turn, look at your cards and see if you can play a card to the right or the left of one of the cards that are on the floor. Right now, because twenty-three is the only card that has been played, can someone tell me which cards could be put next to it?"

Mia piped up, "If you had twenty-four you could put it here." She pointed to the space to the right of card 23. "Because twenty-four comes after twenty-three. Or if you had twenty-two you could put it on the other side."

"I have twenty-two!" Eddie called out.

"OK, Eddie," I said, "Because you have twenty-two, why don't you go first, and then we'll move around the circle and give everyone a turn." Eddie put his 22 card on the floor, right next to the 23. LaVon was sitting next to him, and was anxious to play a card as well.

"What numbers do you have, LaVon?" I asked.

"I've got eighteen and twelve," he reported.

"Do either of those numbers come right before or right after one of the numbers on the floor?" I asked. Most of the children in the circle shook their heads "no."

"So, another way you can play a card is if it is ten more or ten less than a card that's on the floor. Do you have a card that is ten more or ten less than twenty-three or twenty-four?" I asked.

"Yes!" he exclaimed. LaVon jumped up and placed his 12 card above the 22.

I asked, "How did you know so quickly that twelve was ten less than twenty-two?"

"I just looked at the hundreds chart," he replied. "This is like when we built the chart with the cards last week" (LaVon was referring to Lesson L-2 *Building the Hundreds Chart* [*Version 2*].)

"It is like that lesson in a lot of ways," I agreed, "but I want you to watch carefully and let me know if you see a way that today's lesson is different from that lesson."

The next child in the semicircle was Ashley, and she didn't have a card that would fit the rules to play. I explained that if you didn't have a card to play, you can pass. Ashley passed and the game continued around the semicircle. When it was Kayla's turn, the game area looked like this:

```
                        7
      12                       17
20 21 22 23 24 25 26 27 28 29
                     35 36
```

Kayla picked up the 30 card and looked at me quizzically.

"Do I put it after the twenty-nine or under the twenty?"

"That's what makes this a wacky hundreds chart!" I replied. You have a choice about where to place your cards, and your choices determine the shape of the chart we build. It won't always be a rectangle the way our pocket chart is."

Kayla giggled and put the 30 to the right of the 20.

The game continued until all the cards had been played. The game area now looked like this:

```
      2  3  4  5  6  7  8  9 10
     11 12 13 14 15 16 17 18 19
  20 21 22 23 24 25 26 27 28 29 30
                    35 36 37 38 39 40 41 42 43 44
                    45 46 47
```

My students were pleased to have completed the activity successfully. To focus their thinking, I asked one of the lesson's key questions, "How is our wacky hundreds chart different from the hundreds charts we're used to using?" I directed my students to think quietly for a minute, then to turn to their partners and discuss their answer. After giving them a few minutes to talk, I called for their attention again. I repeated the question and called on Joey.

Joey explained, "The hundreds charts we usually use have all straight lines, like straight rows, and this one goes all over the place. Like all the rows on this one aren't the same size."

Rosie said, "On the other charts there's only one place for each number, but, here, sometimes it could go more than one place."

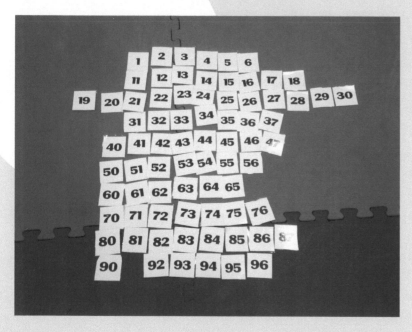

FIGURE L-4.4 A nearly completed wacky hundreds chart.

I understood what Rosie was saying, but I wanted to be sure that everyone in the class did, so I asked Anthony to restate her idea, and use the numbers on the floor to explain what Rosie meant. He pointed to card 45. "This number could have gone next to the forty-four, too, and that would have been OK. Some numbers have more than one spot," he explained.

Next I called on Ashley. "Sometimes it's harder to find a number on the floor. But on the wall you always know where the numbers should be. Can you tell me more about that?" I asked.

"Well, on the wall chart you know that the ten numbers are all in the last column, but on the floor some of them aren't there," she said, pointing to card 20.

"So you mean the numbers you say when you count by tens—ten, twenty, thirty, and so on?" I clarified. Ashley nodded.

One More or One Less

Overview

In this lesson, students become familiar with the numbers one to one hundred represented on the hundreds chart. Using a spinner and number cards, students have the opportunity to add one and subtract one from one- and two-digit numbers. After participating in the whole-class lesson, students get additional practice with the lesson in centers or math stations. The lesson includes a teacher checklist (Reproducible 9) to guide teachers in formative assessment: gathering information about which students are comfortable and which students need more experiences. The lesson is most appropriate for kindergarteners and beginning first graders.

Related Lessons

You might teach the following lesson first:

▶ L-1 Building the Hundreds Chart (Version 1)

Key Questions

▶ How did you know where to place your card?

▶ How can counting out loud help you find the right place to put your one-more (or one-less) card?

▶ How might you find the right pocket for your card without counting from one?

Time

15 minutes, during multiple lessons

Materials

Whole-Group Materials

pocket hundreds chart with removable number cards *or*

interactive whiteboard with a blank 10-by-10 grid projected

a one-more or one-less spinner (Reproducible 2)

Small-Group Materials

copies of The Hundreds Chart (Reproducible A)

Blank Counting Board, 1–20 (Reproducible 3)

Blank Counting Board, 1–30 (Reproducible 4)

Blank Counting Board, 1–50 (Reproducible 5)

Numbered Counting Board, 1–20 (Reproducible 6)

Numbered Counting Board 1–30, for cutting up into number cards (Reproducible 7)

Numbered Counting Board 1–50, for cutting up into number cards (Reproducible 8)

Teacher Checklist: One More or One Less (Reproducible 9)

resealable plastic bags (for storage of center materials)

Technology Tip

Using the Interactive Whiteboard
For this lesson we suggest using a projected 10-by-10 grid rather than an interactive hundreds chart. Many interactive hundreds charts include a feature that, when a space is touched, the number that fits in that space appears. Students should be the ones to touch the numbers.

Teaching Tip

Alternatives to a Spinner
There are many ways to randomize the choices for a student in a game like this. If you prefer not to use a spinner, you could instead use two craft sticks; write *+1* on one stick and *−1* on the other one. Place the sticks in a cup and have students choose one stick. Here are a few other alternatives to a spinner for this game or others like it:

▶ A coin labeled *+1* on one side and *−1* on the other

▶ A die with *+1* written on three sides and *−1* written on the other three sides

▶ A lunch bag with two color tiles, one labeled *+1* and one labeled *−1* (students take a tile from the bag, read it, and replace the tile for the next turn)

▶ Two pieces of paper, one labeled *+1* and one labeled *−1*, folded and placed in a small bowl (students take a piece of paper, read it, and put it back in the bowl for the next turn)

Any of these methods will give students two results, and randomizes the choosing.

Teaching Directions

Whole-Class Lesson

1. Before beginning the lesson, place number cards 1 and 30 in the pocket hundreds chart, then spread out the remaining number cards 2 to 29 in random order, somewhere that is visible to the entire class.

2. Gather students together so they can see the pocket hundreds chart or the projected hundreds chart easily.

3. Ask for two volunteers to come to the front of the group. Explain to the class that the first volunteer will choose a number card, read the number aloud, and place it in the chart. Then, she will spin the spinner and announce whether the spin is one more or one less.

4. The second volunteer then has to find the number card that is *one more* or *one less* (depending on the spin) than the card the first volunteer placed. The second volunteer reads the card and places the appropriate card in the correct pocket on the hundreds chart.

5. Continue to call volunteers to the hundreds chart until all cards have been placed (or until several students grow restless and seem to be ready to move to a different activity!).

Differentiating Your Instruction

Which Numbers Should I Use?

There are a few variables in this lesson that you should consider, depending on your class. One variable is to choose the numbers to use in the initial lesson. Although using the numbers one through thirty is appropriate for many kindergarten classes, some groups of students may need a smaller range of numbers with which to work. Limiting or increasing the numbers used, or the range of numbers, is an easy way to modify the lesson. For example, some students may need to begin with the numbers one through twenty; others may be ready for a greater range of numbers, such as one through fifty. Another differentiation possibility is to eliminate single-digit numbers when students have mastered one more and one less than those numbers.

Choosing to include more anchor numbers from the beginning of the lesson can also differentiate the lesson. The directions call for placing the first and last number in the range before beginning the lesson, but some groups of students may need all the multiples of ten in that range to be included, or possibly one or more multiples of five.

Technology Tip

Using an Interactive Whiteboard

If you choose to use an interactive whiteboard, simply say a number aloud and have the student write the number where it belongs on the projected blank 10-by-10 grid using the interactive pen. However, in doing this you'll miss the opportunity to assess informally students' ability to read the numbers correctly. Consider mixing your approach; use the interactive whiteboard sometimes and, other times, use the pocket chart.

Teaching Tip

Dealing with Incorrect Answers

There are two kinds of incorrect answers a student might give in this lesson. In one case a student may choose a number that is *not* one more or one less than the number at which he is looking. In this case, for example, if a student is looking for the number that is one more than twenty-four and chooses twenty-six, ask him to count aloud from one, and have him slow down his counting when he gets to twenty so he can hear himself say the numbers clearly. If he says, "twenty-four, twenty-six," then you know he doesn't know the order of the numbers. You will need to work with him on this, apart from this lesson.

However, when a wrong answer is given, it is more likely that a student has read the number incorrectly. For instance, David comes to the front and chooses the 17 card, then spins the spinner and gets "one less." His partner, Jordan, then looks for the correct number and, holding up card 61, reads, "Sixteen." In this case, point to cards 13 and 14 (already on the chart) and ask Jordan, "What digit comes first in thirteen and fourteen?" Then redirect Jordan's attention to the number card he is holding and ask him, "Do you notice the difference?" Give students like Jordan every opportunity to self-correct, rather than just telling them the answer. If you can get students to focus on how the numbers are written and to see the pattern that, in this case, numbers in the teens all start with the digit one, they will have a better chance of remembering this pattern than if you simply tell them, "No, that number is sixty-one. Find the number that is a one and a six." Teaching by telling is an ineffective strategy; always seek to help students find the answer with as little direct teaching as possible.

A Child's Mind . . .

Use of a spinner is recommended, or some other way for students to be assigned *one more* or *one less* randomly during this game. When playing the game a few times with first graders, we found that if we give them a choice (either *one more* or *one less*), children always tend to choose one more. They are more comfortable with the forward counting sequence than the backward sequence, especially when the starting point is not a benchmark number, such as ten.

Teaching Tip

If It's Already on the Chart . . .

If a student chooses a number for which the +1 or −1 number is already on the chart, he should go by the results of the alternate spin. For example, cards 13 and 14 are already in the pocket chart. Student 1 spins, gets "one more," and places the number card 15 in the hundred chart. Student 2 spins and gets "one less." Because card 14 is already on the chart, Student 2 should play *one more*, which is card 16.

Teaching Tip

Continuing the Lesson

It is not necessary to place all the cards in one sitting. This activity can be revisited throughout the day or for a couple of days.

Small-Group Lesson

After repeating this lesson with the entire class over the course of several days, place the materials in a center or station so students can continue to experience it in pairs. Offer counting boards for varying ranges of numbers with which to work (1–20, 1–30, and 1–50) instead of a hundreds chart. Be sure to include a completed hundreds chart (Reproducible A) to which students can refer to check themselves. As you observe pairs working, look for opportunities to ask the key questions. Remind students of the rules of the activity:

One More or One Less

1. Student 1 picks a card and finds its place on the hundreds chart.

2. Together, they should check their copy of the hundreds chart to be sure the card is in the correct place.

3. Student 2 spins the spinner, then finds the number card that is *one more* or *one less* (according to the spinner) than the first number card.

4. Together, student pairs should discuss the placement of the card held by Student 2. How do they know the numbers are in the right place? They should use the hundreds chart as needed to help them explain their thinking.

Teaching Tip

Checking Your Work
Allow students to use a completed hundreds chart (Reproducible A) to check their work.

Differentiating Your Instruction

Preparing Materials for Small Groups
To prepare materials for small groups, copy or paste the counting boards and number cards onto cardstock. You might also want to laminate them. Be aware, however, that laminated materials may be difficult for young children to use, because the plastic coating makes the small number cards slip on the counting boards.

As you prepare materials for small groups, think about the differing levels and abilities of your students. What have you noticed as they play the game in a whole group? Offer several counting boards (see the materials list). The number ranges one through thirty and one through fifty are appropriate for most kindergartners, however you may want to have a one-through-twenty counting board available, depending on the abilities of your students. In this way you can pair children by the number range/counting board with which they should be working.

Extend Their Learning!

Placing Both One More and One Less

After the first student chooses a card and places it, the second student must find and place *both* the one-more and one-less cards, unless they are already on the chart.

Matching Number Cards

For students who are having difficulty finding the place for the first card drawn, you may want to begin with a chart that already has several numbers filled in (as stated in "Differentiating Your Instruction" for the whole-group lesson). Then place duplicates of those numbers in a baggie. When the first student chooses a card, he only needs to match the card with the number written on the chart. His partner then spins the spinner and finds the number that goes either before or after that number.

Vary the Type of Spinner

Use a −1 or +1 spinner rather than one with words (see Reproducible 2).

Teacher Reflection

My Experiences with *One More or One Less*

I chose to use the numbers between one and thirty to play this game because, although many of my students can say the counting sequence to one hundred, several are still working on being able to recognize all the two-digit numbers. They are sometimes confused and read the numbers backward. I called on Sarah and Will to come to the front of the group as volunteers. I chose students who I was fairly sure could read the numbers correctly and could use one-to-one correspondence to find the correct place for the number. Sarah chose the card with 26 on it.

"What number did you pick, Sarah?" I asked.

Sarah responded correctly, "Twenty-six." She then began to count, starting with one and touching each space on the chart until she got to twenty-six. She slipped the number card into the chart pocket and spun the spinner, landing on "one more."

"I got one more," Sarah told Will, "You have to find one more than twenty-six."

Will looked through the number cards that I had placed on display, found the 27 card, and put it in the pocket after card 26.

Next I called Paulo and Keisha to the front. Paulo picked card 4 from the spread of numbers on the floor.

"That's easy!" he exclaimed. "It's just, one, two, three, four." He pointed to the number one and the next three spaces after it on the chart. Keisha spun the spinner and this time she landed on "one less." She quickly looked through the numbers on the floor and chose card number 3.

"It's like, one, two, *three,* four," she said, emphasizing the number three. Then she picked up the 5 card and placed it after the 4.

"And this one goes here," she announced. "Three, four, five." She was obviously pleased with herself.

Amauri and Garrett came up as the next volunteers and encountered a bit of a stumbling block. Amauri chose the number 10 card and placed it at the end of the first row. Then she spun "one more." Garrett found the number 11 card, but looked confused about where it should go. He counted aloud from one to eleven to find the correct card to place, but because there wasn't a space to the right of the number 10 card, he initially placed the 11 card in the pocket below the 10 card. Amauri came to his aid.

"It's like in a book," she said. "The next number has to go down to the next row, but back to this side," she said, pointing to the correct space under the number 1 card. Garrett smiled and moved the number card to the place where Amauri was pointing. I wasn't sure that Garrett really understood why the 11 card went where he put it, but rather than try to explain it again myself, I decided to allow Garrett to have more experiences with the hundreds chart and opportunities to see his classmates place more numbers. I knew that if Garrett noticed for himself how numbers are organized as you go from one decade to another, it would be more meaningful to him than if I just told him.

Assessment: One More or One Less

A great way to assess students formatively and to plan for small-group instruction is to use the Teacher Checklist: *One More or One Less* (Reproducible 9) to record strategies observed as students play *One More or One Less*. Copy the checklist and carry it on a clipboard as you circulate around the classroom. Ask students the key questions (listed at the beginning of this lesson) to understand their thinking more completely. Make a note of which students need more experiences with *One More or One Less* and which are ready to move on to other concepts.

Teaching Tip

Teacher Checklists

To learn more about teacher checklists and their valuable role in formative assessment, we recommend the multimedia resource *How to Assess While You Teach Math: Formative Assessment Practices and Lessons* by Dana Islas.

Teacher Checklist: One More or One Less

Student Name and Date	Knew Answer Instantly	Used a Strategy Like Counting from a Benchmark Number	Used the Hundreds Chart	Used the Hundreds Chart and Counted from One	Was Not Able to Find the Correct Number
Sarah Oct. 4	✓ Read 26 with no help				
Will Oct. 4	✓ 27 ✓ read & placed 17.				
Paula Oct. 4		✓ counted back from 20 to 18		✓ to place the #4	
Kesha Oct. 4				✓ to place 3 & 5	
Amauri Oct. 4	✓ placed 10 with no help				
Garrett Oct. 4					
Cora Oct. 4	✓ read and placed 13	✓ started at 10 to get to 12			
Luis Oct. 4				✓ to place 8	
L'Naya Oct. 4	✓ one less than 29	✓ started at 20 to get to 23			✓ one less than 20
Jordan Oct. 4		✓ started at 20 to get to 21		✓ to place 16	

FIGURE L–5.1 A completed teacher checklist for *One More or One Less* (available as Reproducible 9).

Ten More or Ten Less

Overview

This lesson provides a logical sequence for helping students add and subtract ten and multiples of ten to and from any two-digit number. Meant to be repeated several times as students are building their understanding of adding and subtracting tens, the lesson moves learners from using the structure of the hundreds chart to proficient mental arithmetic. The lesson includes a teacher checklist (Reproducible 10) to guide teachers in formative assessment: gathering information about which students are comfortable and which students need more experiences.

Related Lessons

You might teach the following lessons first:

▶ L-3 Arrow Arithmetic

▶ L-2 Building the Hundreds Chart (Version 2)

Consider this lesson as a follow-up:

▶ G-10 How Far Away?

Key Questions

▶ When you look at the hundreds chart, what do you notice?

▶ What happens to the ones place and the tens place?

Time

20 to 30 minutes over the course of several days

Materials

pocket hundreds chart with removable number cards *or*

hundreds chart projected on screen or interactive whiteboard

copies of The Hundreds Chart, one per student (Reproducible A)

transparent markers (refer to the "Materials" section in How To Use This Resource, page xviii)

Teacher Checklist: *Ten More or Ten Less* (Reproducible 10)

Teaching Directions

Day 1

1. Gather students together so they can see the pocket hundreds chart or the projected hundreds chart easily. Make sure the chart has all the number cards in it.

2. Ask students to think about Lesson L-2 *Building the Hundreds Chart* (*Version 2*). Remind them that they placed numbers to the left, right, above, or below a previously placed number. Display and review the sentence frames from L-2.

   Sentence Frames

   ▶ My number is one more than _____ [number].

   ▶ My number is one less than _____ [number].

   ▶ My number is ten more than _____ [number].

   ▶ My number is ten less than _____ [number].

3. Point to card 43 on the chart and ask, "What number is ten more than forty-three?" Highlight the number card and ask the class to whisper the number that is ten more than forty-three. Call on a few volunteers to explain how they knew fifty-three was ten more than forty-three.

   Examples of Student Thinking

   "I counted from forty-three to fifty-three on my fingers."

   "I knew that ten more than forty is fifty, and the three stays the same."

4. Repeat Step 3, each time focusing on ten more than the number you choose. Make sure to highlight the example and the number that is ten more. After four to six examples, pause and ask student to observe

Teaching Tip

Highlighting the Number

If a pocket chart is being used, highlight card 53 with a transparent marker. If an interactive whiteboard is being used, highlight 53 with the interactive pen using the highlighter tool.

the hundreds chart and discuss with a partner what they notice. Call on a few volunteers to share their thinking.

Examples of Student Thinking

"The number that is ten more is always under the starting number."

"The numbers are stacked on each other."

"When I want to know what ten more is, I just look under the number you call out."

5. After students have discussed the patterns they are noticing, ask them to look at the digits in the numbers. First call their attention to the ones place by pointing to number card 43 on the chart and asking, "Which digit is in the ones place?" Then point to card 53 and clarify which digit is in the ones place. Ask students to think about how they would complete the following sentence:

> *When you add ten to a number, the ones place _____.*

Display the sentence for all students to see.

6. Give students a few moments to think before calling on volunteers. Record their responses.

Examples of Student Thinking

"When you add ten to a number, the ones place stays the same."

"When you add ten to a number, the ones place doesn't change."

7. Next call students' attention to the tens place by pointing to number card 43 and asking, "Which digit is in the tens place?" Then point to card 53 and clarify which digit is in the tens place. Ask students to think about how they would complete the following sentence:

> *When you add ten to a number, the tens place _____.*

Display the sentence for all students to see.

Math Matters!

The Value of Ten

Although students may say, "When you add ten to a number, the tens place goes up by one," it is important to be sure they understand that the one in the tens place is actually a ten. Restate what students say to emphasize this point. For example: "You're right. The digit increases by one, and because that digit is in the tens place, the value increased by ten."

8. Give students a few moments to think before calling on a few volunteers. Record their responses.

> **Examples of Student Thinking**
>
> "When you add ten to a number, the tens place goes up by one."
>
> "When you add ten to a number, the tens place gets bigger by one."

9. Pass out copies of the hundreds chart (Reproducible A) to students. Continue to have students practice adding ten by giving them a starting number and having them find the number that is ten more. Each time, remove the markers from the pocket chart or erase the highlights from the interactive whiteboard before giving a new starting number. Have students explain their reasoning for each answer. After practicing several times, some students may be ready to turn their hundreds charts over and practice using mental math to add ten to a two-digit number.

Day 2

10. The next day, begin to ask questions that involve adding twenty or thirty to a number. Follow the same procedure as when adding ten:

    a. Ask students to place a marker on a beginning number.

    b. Give students a multiple of ten to add, such as twenty, thirty, forty, and so on.

    c. Have students place the marker on the sum and whisper the answer to their partner.

    d. Call on volunteers to explain their thinking.

As students explain their thinking, record it on the board using an open number line. For instance, to show 54 + 20 you might show the following:

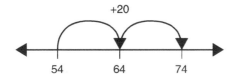

Day 3 and Onward

11. After working on adding ten and multiples of ten for a few days, move to subtracting ten. Follow a similar procedure to adding. Give students a beginning number—for example, eighty-eight—and have them place a transparent marker on that number on the pocket hundreds chart, or highlight 88 if an interactive whiteboard is being used.

12. Ask students to find ten less than that number (if necessary, explain to students that the answer to this problem is called a *difference*). Have students place a transparent marker on the difference, or highlight the difference if an interactive whiteboard is being used.

13. Repeat Steps 11 and 12, each time focusing on ten less than the number you choose. Make sure to highlight the example and the number that is ten less. After four to six examples, pause and ask students to observe the hundreds chart and discuss with a partner what they notice. Call on volunteers to explain how they found the difference.

Examples of Student Thinking

"The number that is ten less is always on top of the number you call out."

"I just look above the number you say on the hundreds chart."

"I just go up the column one box."

Math Matters!

Adding and Subtracting Two-Digit Numbers

To become fluent with adding and subtracting two-digit numbers, students need to be confident in adding multiples of ten to any two-digit number. The time they spend practicing this skill will pay off in increased understanding and fluency with addition and subtraction of multiple-digit numbers.

14. Again, after discussing the patterns students are seeing, look at the digits in the numbers. First call students' attention to the ones place by pointing to card 88 and asking, "Which digit is in the ones place?" Then point to card 78 and clarify which digit is in the ones place. Ask students to think about how they would complete the following sentence:

> *When you subtract ten from a number, the ones place* _____.

Display the sentence for all students to see.

15. After giving them time to think, ask for students to tell how they would complete the sentence.

   Examples of Student Thinking

   "When you subtract ten from a number, the ones places stays the same."

   "When you subtract ten from a number, the ones place doesn't change."

16. Next, call students' attention to the tens place by pointing to card 88 and asking, "Which digit is in the tens place?" Then point to card 78 and clarify which digit is in the tens place. Ask students to think about how they would complete the following sentence:

> *When you subtract ten from a number, the tens place* _____.

Display the sentence for all students to see.

17. After giving them time to think, ask for students to tell how they would complete the sentence.

   Example of Student Thinking

   "When you subtract ten from a number, the tens place goes down by one."

   "When you subtract ten from a number, the tens place is one less than in the number you started with."

18. Pass out copies of The Hundreds Chart (Reproducible A) to students. Continue to have students practice subtracting ten by giving them a starting number and having them find the number that is ten less. Each time, remove the transparent markers from the pocket chart or erase the highlights from the interactive whiteboard before giving the students a new starting number. Have students explain their reasoning for each answer. After practicing several times, some students may be ready to turn over their hundreds charts and practice using mental math to subtract ten from a two-digit number.

19. Continue the lesson the next day, this time asking students to subtract ten, twenty, or thirty.

Extend Their Learning!

Throughout the school year, spend five to ten minutes a few times a week calling out and marking numbers on the hundreds chart and asking students to add or subtract ten to the number. Eventually remove the hundreds chart and call out numbers, asking students to add or subtract ten mentally to the number you have given them.

It Makes Sense! Using the Hundreds Chart to Build Number Sense

54

Teacher Reflection

My Experiences with *Ten More or Ten Less*

Being able to add or subtract ten and multiples of tens from any number increases students' fluency and efficiency when computing numbers mentally. I want students to understand the structure of our number system and be able to use that to their advantage. This lesson focuses students on the ones place staying the same and the tens place increasing or decreasing when adding or subtracting ten and multiples of tens from any number.

By looking at and talking about the geometric pattern this makes on a hundreds chart, students are able create a mental image. I have seen students put their finger up in the air and move it down when asked to add ten to a number. When asked what they're doing, students say they are visualizing a hundreds chart and using their finger to think about what number is under what they are being asked to add ten to.

By looking at and talking about the numerical patterns in the ones and tens place, students realize they need only think about the tens place. I have seen students quickly know the answer when asked to add ten to a number. When asked, students say they added one to the tens place and left the ones place alone.

When I teach this lesson, I send home a note explaining the lesson (consider copying this lesson and sending it home), and ask parents to spend a few minutes each week asking their children to figure out what is *ten more* or *ten less* than numbers they call out. I encourage them to do this when a few free minutes come up, rather than as a formal homework assignment. It can be done while waiting in line at the grocery store, while driving to sports practice, or after eating a family meal.

Assessment: Ten More or Ten Less

A great way to assess students formatively and to plan for small-group instruction is to use a teacher checklist (Reproducible 10) to record strategies observed as students work through the lesson *Ten More or Ten Less*. Copy the checklist and carry it on a clipboard as you circulate around the classroom. Ask students the key questions (listed at the beginning of this lesson) to understand their thinking more completely. I start by asking them to add ten to a few numbers and then subtract ten from a couple of different numbers. If they seem at ease with this, I move to asking them to add or subtract multiples of tens to numbers. Make a note of which students need more experiences with *Ten More or Ten Less* and which are ready to move on to other concepts.

Teaching Tip

Teacher Checklists
To learn more about teacher checklists and their valuable role in formative assessment, we recommend the multimedia resource *How to Assess While You Teach Math: Formative Assessment Practices and Lessons* by Dana Islas.

Teacher Checklist: Ten More or Ten Less

Student Name and Date	Knew Answer Fairly Quickly	Used the Hundreds Chart and Moved in Increments of Ten	Used the Hundreds Chart and Counted by One from the Number	Was Not Able to Find the Correct Number
Jessica 12/2	✓ 10 more than 25	✓ used chart to subtract 10 or 20		
Aaron 12/2		✓ used 100's chart to add or subtract 10s		
Je'Nae 12/2	✓ adds and subtracts easily			
Connor 12/2			✓ still struggling to add or subtract 10's	✓ sometimes not counting accurately
Jordan 12/2		✓ confident in moving up and down chart in groups of ten		
Omar 12/2	✓ adds in his head easily	✓ refers to chart to subtract—needs to work on counting back by tens		
Jennifer 12/2	✓ 10 more than 37 ✓ 20 more than 82 ✓ 10 less than 65			
Yasmin 12/2		✓ moved up and down the hundreds chart to add & subtract	✓ double-checked herself by counting by ones when subtracting	
Max 12/2	✓ very confident when adding or subtracting			

FIGURE L-6.1 A completed teacher checklist for *Ten More or Ten Less* (available as Reproducible 10).

Lesson 7

Hundreds Chart Riddles

Time

10 to 20 minutes

Materials

The Hundreds Chart (1–100) (Reproducible A), one per student

counters to use as markers on the hundreds charts (see How to Use This Resource, page xix, for counter suggestions)

chart paper

Hundreds Chart Riddles: Sets A–C (Reproducible 11)

Overview

In this lesson, the use of riddles provides an engaging avenue for students to develop number relationships, logical reasoning, and communication skills. Riddles also provide an opportunity for students to hear and use mathematical vocabulary (observing the vocabulary students use serves as a kind of formative assessment). The lesson can be taught to the whole class or used as a center (math station) activity or a daily routine.

Related Lessons

You might teach the following lessons and game first:

▶ L-5 One More or One Less

▶ L-6 Ten More or Ten Less

▶ G-1 Number Chart Bingo!

Key Questions

▶ What is your guess? Why?

▶ What do you know about the secret number?

▶ Does the secret number fit our clues?

Teaching Directions

1. Introduce students to the meaning of *riddle*. Ask students, "Have you ever solved a riddle?" Read or display the pet riddle below (record the solutions in Step 2).

The Pet Riddle	Possible Solutions
I could be a pet.	dog, cat, bird, hamster, turtle
I have four legs.	dog, cat, hamster, turtle
I like to run on the wheel in my cage.	hamster

2. After each clue, ask students, "What could the pet be?" Record their thinking. As you move through the riddle, remind students to keep previous clues in mind.

3. Now let students know they will be solving a mathematical riddle using their hundreds chart. Display a demonstration hundreds chart and tell students you've chosen a secret number. Explain that you will reveal clues to help them figure out the secret number. When they hear a clue they should place a counter on a number that they think is the secret number. Pass out copies of the hundreds chart and counters for each student.

4. Display the following riddle, revealing only Clue 1:

Riddle 1

Clue 1: My number is more than 30.

Clue 2: My number is less than 62.

Clue 3: My number is odd.

Clue 4: My number is sum of 20 + 21.

Teaching Tip

What Numbers Should You Use?
Consider using a smaller range of numbers, such as one through thirty or one through fifty, if students are not familiar solving riddles or have not had many experiences using a hundreds chart. Reproducible 11 contains three sets of riddles: Set A is designed for students who are using the number range one through thirty (use Reproducible 7, Numbered Counting Board 1–30), Set B is designed for students who are using the number range one through fifty (use Reproducible 8, Numbered Counting Board 1–50), and Set C is for use with The Hundreds Chart (Reproducible A). For the sake of explanation, this lesson assumes previous use of a hundreds chart in the directions here.

5. Read Clue 1, then ask students, "What could the secret number be?" Have four to five students volunteer their thinking and verify that all students have placed a counter on a number. Record their responses next to the first clue:

Riddle 1	Possible Solutions
Clue 1: *My number is* *more than 30.*	*31, 100, 55, 72, 38*

6. Read Clue 2 and ask students to move their counters on their hundreds chart if necessary.

7. To make sure students are using both clues, have students turn to their partners and share two facts thus far revealed about the secret number.

8. Ask one student to share the two facts with the whole class, and have students check one more time to confirm that their marker is on a number that fits both facts.

9. Circulate, checking students' hundreds charts. If a student is incorrect, do not tell her how to fix it. Instead, repeat each clue and ask if the marker is on a number that fits the facts.

10. Bring the students' attention back to the displayed riddle. Ask students, "What could the secret number be?" Record their responses next to the second clue.

Riddle 1	Possible Solutions
Clue 1: *My number is* *more than 30.*	*31, 100, 55, 72, 38*
Clue 2: *My number is* *less than 62.*	*31, 59, 42, 40, 37*

A Child's Mind . . .

It can be difficult for young learners to hold two or three disparate pieces of information in their mind at one time. A child may move her marker to forty-eight, which is more than thirty, but then move her marker to twenty-two, which is less than sixty-two, and may not remember that the number must also be more than thirty.

11. Read Clue 3. Ask students, "What do you know about odd numbers?" Have them turn to their partners and share what they know. Ask a few students to share their thinking with the whole class.

12. Ask students, "What could the secret number be?" Remind students that their solution must fit the first three facts. Give them time to move their counters.

13. Ask a few students to share their solutions with the class. Record their responses next to the third clue.

Riddle 1	Possible Solutions
Clue 1: My number is more than 30.	31, 100, 55, 72, 38
Clue 2: My number is less than 62.	31, 59, 42, 40, 37
Clue 3: My number is odd.	31, 43, 59, 55, 35

14. Ask students, "Could twenty-five be a solution? Why or why not?" Have them turn to their partner and discuss their thinking.

15. Call on a student to share her answer with the class.

16. Repeat Steps 14 and 15 two more times using the numbers sixty-six and forty-four.

17. Finally, read Clue 4: *My number is the sum of 20 + 21.* Give students time to think about the clue and move their counters. Ask them to whisper the solution.

18. Tell students you want to restate the clues to make sure forty-one fits all the clues. Read a clue by inserting *forty-one* into the sentence. For example, "Forty-one is more than thirty." Give students a few moments to think before asking them if the statement is true.

Differentiating Your Instruction

Modifying the Lesson
If the majority of the class is struggling, bring the students to the whole-group area and display a hundreds chart and the two clues. Call out a number and ask if the number is more than thirty and discuss it. Ask if the number is less than sixty-two and discuss it. Continue with a few more numbers—ones that fit both clues and ones that don't—before continuing with the lesson.

Teaching Tip

Connecting to the Symbol
Consider writing *41 is greater than 30* with symbols—*41 > 30*—in addition to the words. Continue this for each clue that lends itself to writing with symbols.

Extend Their Learning!

Create a Riddle

Create your own riddle (see the structure and steps presented here) or use riddles from Reproducible 11. Revisit the riddles on subsequent days.

Structure for Writing Riddles

1. Pick a number on the hundreds chart. Write four clues as follows:

   Clue 1: Use a comparison statement with the terms *more than*, *greater than*, *less than*, or *smaller than*.

   Clue 2: Use a comparison statement that includes the opposite of the statement used during the first clue.

   Clue 3: Include a skill on which you want to work, like odd/even or skip-counting.

   Clue 4: Use addition or subtraction.

2. After students are familiar with solving riddles, display the Structure For Writing Riddles and explain that students will create their own riddles for their peers to solve.

3. Tell students they must first pick a number on the hundreds chart. Call on a volunteer to choose a number to begin the demonstration. Record the number or highlight the number on the chart.

4. Next point to the directions for writing the first clue and read it aloud to the class. Give a few examples for students before calling on a student to share a statement. Record it on chart paper.

5. Continue in this way for the next three clues: read the directions for writing the clue out loud, give a few examples, and call on a student to share a statement. Record the statements to create a class riddle.

Teaching Tip

Ideas for Clues

Clue 3 can be challenging to write. Here are a few examples to get you started:

My number has a 4 in the 10s place.

My number has a 1 in the 1s place.

My number is 1 away from a decade number.

You do not say my number when you skip-count by 5s.

6. Ask whether students have any questions before sending them back to their seats to create riddles. Give students a set amount of time to write as many riddles as they can. Move from student to student, helping when needed and reviewing their riddles.

7. Call the students to the whole-group area and model how to read a riddle correctly while others try to solve it. Remind students that the reader is to read one clue at a time, pausing to allow the guessers to make one guess.

8. Group students in threes or fours and ask them to share their riddles while their peers try to solve them.

9. Collect the riddles from students and place them in an area of the room where they will be accessible for students during center time, or when they have free-choice time.

Teacher Reflection

My Experiences with *Hundreds Chart Riddles*

I have always found riddles to be highly engaging for students and easily implemented by teachers. You don't need a lot of materials, and students get really excited the closer they come to solving the riddle. I love that you can personalize riddles to fit the needs of your class by choosing to write clues based on the skills and concepts on which you want to focus. I think it is very beneficial to pause after each clue and take a few guesses from students. When you discuss their guesses with the class, you gain insight into student thinking. I also believe it is important to connect the correct guess with the clues at the end of the riddle. This helps all children understand that the correct answer wasn't just a guess, but a number that fit a specific set of criteria. Whenever possible, I also make sure I write the clue in symbolic form to connect the words and symbols.

Riddles can be implemented as a routine (something you do the first five to ten minutes of class), a whole-class lesson, a small-group activity, or a quick activity when you have an extra five to ten minutes. When I'm tutoring groups, I often start with solving riddles, which helps make students feel comfortable. Riddles also work great for family math nights. Start by displaying premade riddles and having parents solve them with their children, then ask each family to write their own. Riddles are extremely versatile; you and your students will enjoy them however you choose to use them.

Assessment: Hundreds Chart Riddles

When we think about what we want for our students in terms of mathematical vocabulary, most of us would agree that we want our students to understand the vocabulary when they hear or read it, as well as be able to use it orally and in writing. Riddles provide an excellent opportunity for students to use the vocabulary they've been learning in class. When they use the vocabulary correctly, we can be sure that they understand it. In this way, riddles can be seen as a type of formative assessment. Reading students' riddle will let you know which vocabulary they really understand.

Lesson 8

Look, Quick!

Overview

In this lesson, a partially colored in 10-by-10 grid is shown to students for a few seconds. Students determine how many squares are colored in by using the benchmark numbers of five, ten, and fifty. The lesson develops students' ability to see and recognize groups of numbers instead of always counting by ones. The ability to see groups of objects is known as subitizing.

Related Lessons

You might teach the following lesson first:

▶ L-1 Building the Hundreds Chart (Version 1)

Key Questions

▶ How many squares are colored in? How do you know?

Time

first use: 20 minutes

additional uses (as a routine during the year): 5–10 minutes

Materials

10-by-10 grid (Reproducible D)

writing utensil with which you can easily color in the grid and erase

Teaching Directions

1. Gather students in a whole-group area and display a 10-by-10 grid. Count the rows and columns with students to determine the total number of squares on the grid.

2. Explain that you will color in some rows and a few leftover squares. Tell students they need to determine how many squares have been colored in, but they can only see the grid for a few seconds. Explain that you will mark the chart to show some bench-mark numbers that will help them quickly *see* how much is colored in.

3. Count over five squares and draw a vertical line down the grid.

10-by-10 Grid (Reproducible D)

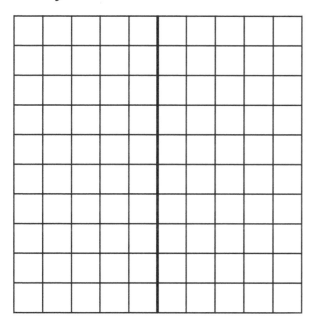

4. Next, color in fifteen squares (the top row and the first five squares on the second row), but don't let students watch as you do this!

A Child's Mind . . .

Rows or Columns?

Some students may want to count the rows by tens whereas others may want to count the columns by ten. Often students won't realize until they try it that the total is the same whether they count the rows or the columns. Compare the 10-by-10 grid with a hundreds chart and discuss the similarities and differences.

Math Matters!

Subitizing

The ability to glance at a group of objects and see quickly how many there are without counting them one by one (see *Math Matters: Understanding the Math You Teach, Grades K–8*, 2nd edition, by Suzanne H. Chapin and Art Johnson [2006, Math Solutions]).

5. Show the grid to the class now for modeling purposes only; allow them to see it for as long as necessary. Ask, "How does the dark line help you see what's been colored in?"

   Examples of Student Thinking

   "I know a full row is ten and the dark line means you colored in five, so it's fifteen."

   "I see ten and five and that's fifteen. The dark line told me it was five colored in."

6. Now color in twenty-six squares (the first two top rows and the first five squares on the third row). Once again, do not let students see you doing this!

FIGURE L-8.1 Here the grid is displayed to the class using a document camera. There are twenty-six squares colored in.

7. Show the grid to the class and ask, "How does the dark line help you see what's been colored in?"

   Examples of Student Thinking

   "I know two rows is twenty and I saw one square past the dark line was colored in, so that's six. Twenty and six is twenty-six."

   "I saw twenty and then the next row I saw five first and added one more because one more past the dark line was colored in. So that's twenty-six."

FIGURE L-8.2 Mrs. Conklin asks the question, "How does the dark line help you see what's been colored in?" and listens as students respond.

8. Explain that we have a benchmark for fives and you would like to add a benchmark for fifty. Count by tens until you reach the fiftieth square and draw a horizontal black line.

10-by-10 Grid (Reproducible D)

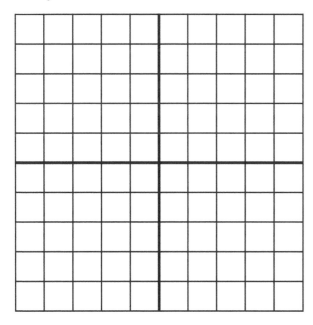

A Child's Mind . . .

Give Me a Thumbs Up

Look, Quick! is often very exciting for students, and they have a hard time not waiting their turn to share what they saw. You might find that your students shout out the answer. Before the grid is shown, remind students gently to be quiet and to keep what they see to themselves. In my classroom, I ask students to give me a thumbs-up when they know how many squares have been colored in.

Technology Tip

Using the Interactive Whiteboard or Other Projection Device

Allow students to look for about three to five seconds, then cover the grid with the shade feature if an interactive whiteboard is being used, or cover the grid with paper if an overhead or document camera is being used.

Teaching Tip

Pacing

Some classes may benefit from simple numbers being colored in for several days before they are comfortable moving on to more complex numbers.

9. Now color in seventy and ask, "How does the dark line help you see what's been colored in?"

Examples of Student Thinking

"I know fifty was colored in because I saw every square above the dark line was colored in, and then I counted by tens to seventy."

"I saw that fifty squares were colored in and added two more rows which is twenty. Fifty and twenty is seventy."

10. Remind students that you will color in some squares and they will be given a few seconds to determine how many squares are colored in. Encourage them to use the benchmarks of five and fifty.

11. Start with simple numbers like fifteen, thirty-five, forty, and sixty so students can become familiar with the format of having to look quickly, and can also begin using the benchmarks. After each number is shown, ask students the key questions: "How many squares are colored in? How do you know?"

12. Move on to more complex numbers. Color in thirty-three squares, show the class, and ask for volunteers to share how many squares they believe are colored in. Encourage them to explain how they knew what was colored in, and you record their thinking using equations.

Examples of Student Thinking and Teacher Recording

Student says: "I knew the first three rows is thirty and then I counted by ones: thirty-one, thirty-two, thirty-three."

Teacher records: $30 + 1 + 1 + 1 = 33$

Student says: "I saw thirty. Then I saw it was almost to the five line but it was two away so that's three. Thirty and three is thirty-three."

Teacher records: *30 + (5 − 2) = 33* or *30 + 3 = 33*

13. Continue coloring more complex numbers and connecting student thinking to the matching equations.

14. After several sessions of *Look, Quick!*, ask students to explain how the benchmark numbers of five and fifty help them see quickly how many squares are colored in.

Teaching Tip

Using Parentheses When Recording
Consider using parentheses when it connects to student's thinking. Explain to students that it's a way mathematicians record their thinking if a lot of things are going on. As you record the parentheses, say something like, "This tells us that we should subtract the two from the five before adding the three to the thirty." Don't necessarily expect students to start using parentheses, but do expose them to the mathematical way of representing their thinking. If using parentheses is uncomfortable for you, simply draw a thought bubble to record the child's thinking. Either way, the goal remains the same: putting student thinking down on paper so they can connect what they think to the mathematical symbols.

Extend Their Learning!

Give students the opportunity to do play *Look, Quick!* on their own, in pairs. Provide partners with a laminated 10-by-10 grid and a dry erase marker. First model a few rounds with a student volunteer. Ask the student volunteer to cover her eyes or turn around so she can't see as you color in some squares. Remind everyone that the coloring doesn't have to be perfect; they just need to swipe their dry erase marker through the rows, being more careful to color in the leftover squares. Have the volunteer turn around and look at the grid as you slowly count to three. Then ask the key questions: "How many squares are colored in? How do you know?" Post the key questions in the room so students can refer to them when they are playing with a partner.

Erase the markings from the grid and pass it to the volunteer. Repeat the series of steps until students understand how to work with a partner.

FIGURE L-8.3 First grader Karina colors in squares on her hundreds chart while her partner, Aaron, covers his eyes to ensure he's not looking!

FIGURE L-8.4 Aaron thinks about how to explain to Karina the number of squares colored in.

Missing Number Puzzles

Overview

In this lesson, students work with puzzles that are pieces of a hundreds chart. The focus, which is on just a portion of the chart, helps students concentrate on where a particular number is in relation to the numbers around it. Students think about how the numbers on the chart are related, both by tens in columns and by ones in rows.

Related Lessons

You might teach the following lessons first:

▶ L-1 Building the Hundreds Chart (Version 1)

▶ L-2 Building the Hundreds Chart (Version 2)

▶ L-4 Building a Wacky Hundreds Chart

Consider this game as a follow-up:

▶ G-5 Don't Get Lost

Key Questions

▶ Where do you start on a new puzzle? Is there one square on each puzzle that makes a better starting place than the others?

▶ Are any of the puzzles harder than others? Which ones? Why?

▶ What shapes are the easiest puzzles?

Time

30 to 40 minutes

Materials

Missing Number Puzzles (Reproducible 12, Sets 1–4) copied on cardstock or other stiff paper, laminated, and cut out

dry-erase markers, one for each pair of students (for puzzle option)

Missing Number Puzzles (Reproducible 12, 1 of Sets 1–4), 1 copy per student (for worksheet option)

Missing Number Puzzles Assessment (Reproducible 13), 1 per student

Teaching Directions

Introduce

1. Gather students together to introduce the lesson. Begin with the puzzle in the shape of a plus sign (see Reproducible 12, Set 3). Project or place the enlarged version of this puzzle where all students can see it.

2. Explain to students, "This is a puzzle piece for a game you're going to play today called *Missing Number Puzzles.* Can you tell what this piece is a part of? Does it remind you of anything?"

   Examples of Student Thinking

   "It looks like a plus with forty-two in the middle."

   "I think it looks like a T, but there's a number in the middle."

   If students do not connect it with a hundreds chart, explain, "This is a small part of a hundreds chart. It looks like I just copied this one tiny piece, but I erased all the numbers around the forty-two."

3. Tell students that their job is to decide which numbers are missing from each piece of the chart and fill them in.

4. Ask for a student volunteer to fill in one of the empty boxes on the puzzle and to explain how she knows which number goes there.

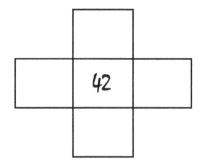

   Example of Student Thinking

   "I know that forty-one comes before forty-two, so it goes in the box before forty-two."

5. Continue eliciting numbers for the puzzle until it is complete. Each time a student fills in a number, ask her to explain her thinking.

Examples of Student Thinking

"I think forty-three goes after the forty-two, because that's what you say when you count: forty-one, forty-two, forty-three."

"I know that thirty-two goes on top of forty-two because it's like when we played the *Wacky Hundreds Chart* game (L-4). When the number is ten less it goes on top of the other number."

Explore

6. Now it's the students' turn to work in pairs and complete the puzzles. Hand out two laminated puzzles for every pair of students, along with a dry-erase marker (or hand out copies of one of the entire sets in Reproducible 12).

7. Explain that students will work together to fill in the missing numbers. Next, they will use a hundreds chart to check their puzzle to be sure they have filled in the correct numbers. Last, students will erase their puzzles before returning them to a central location and choosing two more puzzles on which to work.

8. Display Directions for Missing Number Puzzles for everyone to see.

Directions for Missing Number Puzzles

1. Fill in the numbers on your puzzles.

2. Check your puzzle by looking at a complete hundreds chart.

3. Erase the numbers on your puzzles.

4. Return your puzzles and choose two more.

9. Circulate in the classroom as students are working on their puzzles. Ask the key questions listed at the beginning of this lesson.

Teaching Tip

Options for Practice

There are two options for students' independent practice with Missing Number Puzzles. One option is simply to photocopy the sets in Reproducible 12 and have students work alone or with a partner to fill in the missing numbers on their "worksheets." A second option is to reproduce the same sets on heavy paper, laminate them, and cut out the individual puzzles. Then have students record on the puzzles using a dry-erase marker. In this way, students concentrate on one puzzle at a time and, because the puzzles are nonconsumable, you can put them in a center to be solved again later.

Teaching Tip

Assessment

After the Missing Number Puzzles have been in your math stations for two weeks or so, you may want to use Missing Number Puzzles Assessment (Reproducible 13) as an assessment to determine how well your students are able to use what they know about the hundreds chart to fill in the missing numbers.

Summarize

10. After students have had the chance to complete at least three puzzles, call them back together. Use the key questions to lead a short discussion about how the puzzles relate to previous lesson experiences (L-1 *Building the Hundreds Chart* (*Version 1*), L-2 *Building the Hundreds Chart* (*Version 2*), and L-4 *Building a Wacky Hundreds Chart*).

11. Explain to the class that the puzzles will be put in a center (math station) for future exploration. Although students may have solved several of the puzzles, they benefit from repeating mathematical experiences several times, and often deepen their understanding the second or third time they work on a puzzle.

Teacher Reflection

My Experiences with *Missing Number Puzzles*

I introduced Missing Number Puzzles with the puzzle that looks like a plus sign. I drew it on the easel, large enough for the class to see, with boxes big enough to write inside. This puzzle is simple in that it involves moving straight up and down one column and across one row, in the same way most of the previous lessons and games do. I asked students, "Can you tell where it looks like this puzzle came from? Does it remind you of anything?"

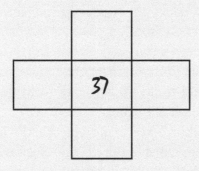

Tia responded, "It looks like a piece of the hundreds chart cut out!"

I then asked, "What numbers do you think should go in the squares?" I gave the class a few minutes to think about their answers, and then I called on Ben.

"I think next to the thirty-seven should be thirty-eight; on the right side, because thirty-eight comes after thirty-seven," Ben declared.

Several students nodded to indicate their agreement, so I had Ben come up and write *38* on the puzzle.

Shazia spoke next. "So on the other side it should be thirty-six, so it goes thirty-six, thirty-seven, thirty-eight across."

Shazia came up and wrote *36* in the box next to the thirty-seven.

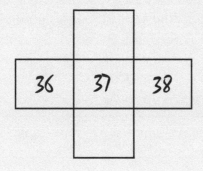

I asked the class if they agreed with Shazia's thinking.

Diamond said, "I agree with Shazia and Ben. Now it looks like part of the hundreds chart with the corners missing."

"What do you think should go in this box and why do you think that?" I asked, pointing to the box above thirty-seven.

Demetrius raised his hand. "I think it's twenty-seven because it's just like the *Arrow Arithmetic* game. When you go up in a column it's ten. I counted thirty-seven, thirty-six, thirty-five, thirty-four, thirty-three," Demetrius explained as he kept track with his fingers, "thirty-two, thirty-one, thirty, twenty-nine, twenty-eight, twenty-seven." He pointed triumphantly at the box and wrote *27* above the thirty-seven. (**Note:** The game to which Demetrius is referring is Lesson L-3, *Arrow Arithmetic*.)

"So that means forty-seven goes under thirty-seven because it's ten more," Kiara said. "That finishes the puzzle!"

"What could we use to check ourselves to be sure we've filled in the puzzle correctly?" I inquired further.

"We could just look at a real hundreds chart," Nia suggested. Because I have a basket with laminated hundreds charts always available to students at the front of the room, we quickly passed out the charts and agreed that the puzzle was filled in correctly.

I then directed students to turn their hundreds charts face down on the floor before starting the next puzzle. I showed students the following:

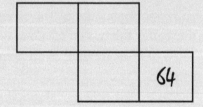

"Here's another puzzle with just one number in it. It's a piece of the hundreds chart, just like the last puzzle. You have to figure out what numbers go in the other spaces. Who wants to tell us a number that fits into this puzzle?" I asked. I gave everyone a few quiet moments to think, then called on Grace.

"I think sixty-three goes next to sixty-four, because it's one less than sixty-four," Grace mused.

Nia nodded and added, "And fifty-three goes on top of sixty-three. It's ten less than sixty-three."

Trevon finished the puzzle by writing *52* in the last empty square.

I assigned each student a partner with whom to work and passed out two laminated puzzles and one dry-erase marker to each pair. I explained that partners needed to discuss how to fill in the puzzle before using the dry-erase marker. I reminded them to check their work by looking at a hundreds chart when they were finished, then they needed to clean off the laminated puzzles and come get two more from the basket filled with extra puzzles. The students eagerly got to work while I circulated around the room, observing and asking key questions.

Lesson 10 From Here to There: Solving Comparison Problems

Time

one to three class periods

Materials

The Hundreds Chart (Reproducible A), enlarged for whole-class use

For One-Digit Differences

counters, to be used for one-digit differences (see How to Use This Resource, page xix)

pocket hundreds chart with removable number cards *or*

a hundreds chart projected on screen or using an interactive whiteboard

transparent markers (see How To Use This Resource, page xviii)

For Two-Digit Differences

pocket hundreds chart with removable number cards *or*

hundreds chart projected on screen or interactive whiteboard

transparent markers (see How To Use This Resource, page xviii)

From Here to There Word Problems (Reproducible 14)

The Hundreds Chart (Reproducible A), one per student

Overview

This lesson focuses on finding the difference between two numbers on the hundreds chart. Directions are given at two levels: one-digit differences (counters drawn from a bag) and two-digit differences (the contexts of temperature differences in two cities). Students use a hundreds charts to subtract or add to determine the difference. Explicit modeling by you, the teacher, gives students new tools for recording their thinking.

Related Lessons

You might teach the following lessons and game first:

▶ L-5 One More or One Less

▶ L-6 Ten More or Ten Less

▶ G-10 How Far Away?

Key Questions

▶ What is the difference?

▶ Does it matter which number is used to start?

▶ What is similar about the strategies that are recorded?

Teaching Directions

One-Digit Differences

1. Gather students in the whole-group area and refer to the hundreds chart. Tell students they are going to solve problems using the chart and also using counters as tools to help them.

2. Put the counters in a resealable bag and have students watch as you take a handful from the bag. Place the counters in a row and ask students to count to find the total. Mark the number on the hundreds chart.

3. Ask a student to reach into the bag and take a handful of counters. As you or your students place the counters in a row above the teacher's row of counters, have the class count to find the total of the student's row. Mark the number on the hundreds chart.

4. Ask the class to point quietly to the row of counters that has the most. Think aloud by saying, "I wonder how many more counters I have?" Point to the rows, showing students that the first several counters in each row are equal. Point to the remainder of your row, telling students that you have more counters and want to count to find out how many more (or less, depending on the number of counters the student drew from the bag).

5. Have the class count with you to determine how many more counters you have. Restate this finding in a complete sentence, "I have [number] more counters than [student's name]."

6. Refer to the hundreds chart and demonstrate how to count on from the student's number. For example, if the student pulled eight counters from the bag and you pulled out fifteen, use a transparent marker to mark both numbers on the pocket hundreds chart, or mark both numbers on the chart you are projecting. Then ask students to help you count on

Teaching Tip

Using a Partially Filled Chart
Consider showing only the numbers one through twenty because the problems do not use larger numbers. Showing only one through twenty allows students to focus on just those numbers.

Teaching Tip

Marking the Hundreds Chart
To mark a pocket hundreds chart, use a transparent marker. Transparent markers for the pocket hundreds chart are commercially available through math catalogs or can be made by cutting squares from a colored transparency the same size as the removable cards. As an alternative, you can cut small rectangles of construction paper that are slightly larger than the removable cards to place behind the numbers to which you want to draw attention. (For example, if the number card is 1.5 by $\frac{1}{5}$ inches, cut the rectangle to be 1.5 by 2 inches, so that the construction paper sticks up above the top of the number card just a bit.) For hundreds charts on interactive whiteboards, document cameras, or the overhead, color the appropriate square yellow.

Math Matters!

What Is Being Counted?

Often children make the mistake of counting the number they are on as they count to find the difference between two numbers. It's important to model for them that what is being counted is the *space* between the numbers, or the number of jumps it takes to get from one number to the next.

Teaching Tip

When Should I Introduce Recording?

After students are comfortable using the counters or hundreds chart to find the difference, introduce how to record their thinking. This activity could occur several days after the initial lesson or the next day, depending on your students. Listen to how students solve the problem, and record their solution so they can begin to see the connections between what they say and what it looks like on paper.

from eight to fifteen. Be sure to model, saying the counting word as you move your finger from number to number. Remind students that you are counting the number of jumps, or steps, it takes to get from one number to another on the chart. Finally, restate the finding in a complete sentence. For example, "I have seven more counters than Tia."

7. Sum up the experience thus far by telling students that one can find how many more counters a person has by counting on a hundreds chart or using the counters.

8. Remove the counters the student selected and have another student take a handful of counters from the bag. Repeat the sequence, using the counters and hundreds chart to find the difference.

9. When students are comfortable using the counters and the chart to solve a problem, introduce a method for recording their thinking. Grab a handful of counters, place them in a row, and have a student do the same. Just like before, use the counters to solve the problem. In this case, let's say you pull eight counters and a student pulls four.

10. Tell students you would like to show them how to record their thinking. Draw the two sets of counters. Explain that we counted on, saying, "One, two, three, four," as you record *1 2 3 4* under the counters you've drawn.

Example of Teacher Recording

Mrs. C's counters:

☐ ☐ ☐ ☐ ☐ ☐ ☐ ☐

Student's counters:

☐ ☐ ☐ ☐ 1 2 3 4

11. Tell students the recording matches their thinking if they used the counters to solve the problem. Now tell them you would like to show them how to record their thinking if they used the hundreds chart.

12. Solve the problem with the class using the hundreds chart. For example, if you take twelve counters out of the bag and the student takes eight counters, mark the numbers *8* and *12*. Point to numbers nine, ten, eleven, and twelve on the hundreds chart as you count the difference, "One, two, three, four." Remind students that you are counting the number of jumps between the two marked numbers. Then draw a partial hundreds chart. Explain that you counted on, saying, "One, two, three, four" as you record *1 2 3 4* under the partial hundreds chart.

Example of Teacher Recording

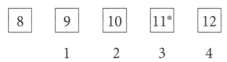

13. Conclude by reminding students they can use the counters *or* hundreds chart to solve the problem.

14. Revisit this lesson as needed.

Two-Digit Differences

1. Tell students they will be solving problems about the weather and you would like them to talk with their partner about the weather outside. Prompt them with a few questions such as, "Is it hot or cold? Is it sunny or cloudy?"

2. Next, tell students the temperature (either Google it or do research ahead of time). Mark the temperature on the hundreds chart.

Teaching Tip

Marking the Hundreds Chart
To mark a pocket hundreds chart, use a transparent marker. Transparent markers for the pocket hundreds chart are commercially available through math catalogs or can be made by cutting squares from a colored transparency the same size as the removable cards. As an alternative, you can cut small rectangles of construction paper that are slightly larger than the removable cards to place behind the numbers to which you want to draw attention. (For example, if the number card is 1.5 by $\frac{1}{5}$ inches, cut the rectangle to be 1.5 by 2 inches, so that the construction paper sticks up above the top of the number card just a bit.) For hundreds charts on interactive whiteboards, document cameras, or the overhead, color the appropriate square yellow.

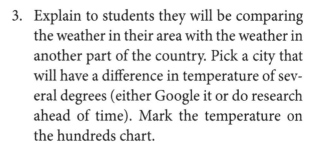

3. Explain to students they will be comparing the weather in their area with the weather in another part of the country. Pick a city that will have a difference in temperature of several degrees (either Google it or do research ahead of time). Mark the temperature on the hundreds chart.

4. Help students connect to the temperatures by discussing what kinds of clothes students are wearing in their classroom and predicting what people are wearing in the other city.

5. Ask, "What's the difference between the temperatures in the two cities?" Explain that the word *difference* means how far apart the numbers are. Give students time to think about the question; have hundreds charts available for those students who need them.

6. When everyone seems ready, ask students to share with their partner how they solved the problem. Then call on a volunteer to share her thinking while you record it. For modeling purposes here, let's say the two temperatures are seventy-two and ninety-four.

   Example of Student Thinking: Addition Strategy

   "I started with the seventy-two and counted by tens to ninety-two, so I said ten, twenty. Then I moved from ninety-two to ninety-four and said twenty-one, twenty-two. The difference is twenty-two."

Examples of How the Teacher Could Record Student Thinking: Addition

Partial Hundreds Chart

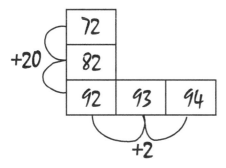

Open Number Line

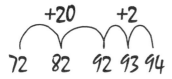

Partial Sums

$$72 + \boxed{20} = 92$$
$$92 + \boxed{2} = 94$$

Teaching Tip

Which Way Do I Record?

The three methods of recording shown here are all appropriate to illustrate a student's thinking. If a student calculates the difference mentally, use an open number line or partial sums. If a student comes up to the hundreds chart and points to the numbers, use a partial hundreds chart. Students will eventually tell you the way they would like for you to record—after they've been introduced to the methods!

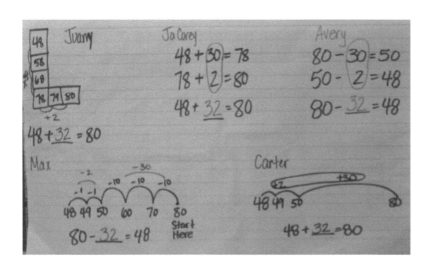

FIGURE L-10.1 Mrs. Conklin engaged the class in a discussion about the similarities and differences of the strategies in recording in the hope that students would make connections between addition and subtraction. Here we see the recordings.

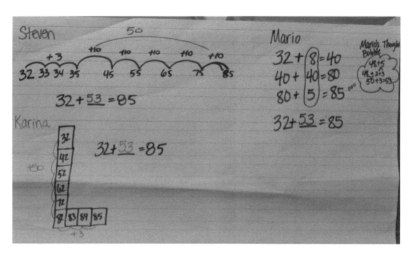

FIGURE L-10.2 This is another sample recording done in Mrs. Conklin's classroom. The student, Mario, explained how he added the circled numbers: "I knew that forty and eight was forty-eight. I split five into two and three, so forty-eight plus two was fifty, and three more is fifty-three." Although Mario hadn't written this down, Mrs. Conklin recorded his thinking as a thought bubble so the whole class could see his strategy of splitting the five to add it easily to forty-eight.

Teaching Tip

Students Who Repeat Strategies

If a student repeats a solution strategy, you can take one of two approaches. First, allow him to finish, and then ask if his strategy matches a strategy that has already been recorded. When the student finds the strategy that matches his thinking, thank him for reiterating the strategy. Second, allow him to finish and ask, "Does that strategy match one that has already been recorded?" Then ask if the student would like it recorded using a different method. For example, if an open number line has been used, a student may want the strategy to be recorded using the hundreds chart method.

7. Restate or have another student restate the student's thinking as you record a matching number sentence. Example: "We started on seventy-two so I'll record 'seventy-two,' and then we added to ninety-four. I'm going to record a plus and a line because we didn't know what we added until we were finished. I'll record 'equals ninety-four.' When we finished, we found out we added twenty-two, so I'll fill in the blank addend with the number twenty-two."

$$72 + \underline{22} = 94$$

8. Call on another volunteer to share her thinking while you record. Then restate or have another student restate the volunteer's thinking while you record a matching number sentence.

9. Call on another volunteer to share her thinking. If no one has started from the larger number and subtracted to the smaller number, ask the class to solve the problem using subtraction. Call on a volunteer to share her thinking while you record.

Example of Student Thinking: Subtraction

"I started with ninety-four and counted to seventy-four by tens. I said, 'Ten, twenty.' Then I counted back to seventy-two and said, 'Twenty-one, twenty-two.' The difference is twenty-two."

Examples of How the Teacher Could Record Student Thinking: Subtraction

Partial Hundreds Chart

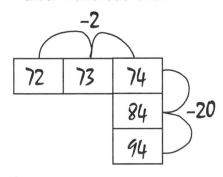

Open Number Line

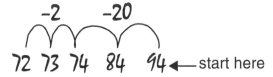

72 73 74 84 94 ←— start here

Partial Difference

$$94 - \boxed{20} = 74$$
$$74 - \boxed{2} = 72$$

A Child's Mind . . .

Addition or Subtraction?
Most students feel more comfortable with addition. Although adding is an efficient method for solving the problem, we want students to see the connections between addition and subtraction, which is why it's important to ask them to solve using subtraction.

Teaching Tip

How Many Students Do I Call On?
Call on enough students to gain a variety of strategies. If you listen to students when they share their solution strategies with their partner, you can call on those students with differing methods. You want at least one strategy in which a student has added to the larger number and at least one strategy in which a student has subtracted to the smaller number so that you can compare and discuss the results.

10. Have a class discussion. Ask students to look at the strategies and consider the key questions listed here.

Key Questions for Class Discussion

▶ What is the difference?

▶ Did it matter which number you started with?

▶ What is similar about the strategies you see recorded?

11. Repeat this lesson on subsequent days so students have opportunities to become more efficient at finding the difference and making connections between addition and subtraction.

12. When the class is ready to record their own thinking, pass out copies of the From Here to There Word Problems (Reproducible 14) and The Hundreds Chart (Reproducible A).

Differentiating Your Instruction

When Students Finish Step 12 Early
List several cities and their temperatures where all students can see. If students finish the lesson early, ask them to pick two cities and find the difference in temperatures. Have them repeat this several times until the remainder of the students finish the word problems.

Teacher Reflection

My Experiences with *From Here to There*: Scribing Students' Strategies

Scribing students' strategies not only helps students learn how to record their own ways of thinking, it also provides us with valuable information about how our students are thinking.

Before calling on students to scribe their thinking, observe them and make a note of different solution methods; your recording sheet then becomes a complete record of all the ways students are thinking of solving the problem. Next, call on three to four students, starting with the least sophisticated solution method, which will help those students who are still working use more efficient solution strategies.

As you continue to call on others to share their strategies, you might ask, "Do you notice anything that is the same about these strategies? Do you notice anything different about them?" Questions such as these are key to helping students analyze their own strategies, see the similarities among all of the different strategies, and make it easier for students to adopt more sophisticated strategies.

Another important aspect of scribing student strategies is connecting students' mental arithmetic to correct mathematical notation. As students describe their strategies, check in often to be sure that what you are recording matches their thinking. Ask,

▶ "Is this what you were thinking as you solved the problem?"

▶ "Look at this and tell me if it matches what you did in your head."

If students indicate that your scribing doesn't match their thinking, try scribing for them again. Often students solve problems in their heads and aren't really aware of the steps they took; by scribing for them on the board, you are essentially putting their thinking in slow motion so that they will become aware of the steps they took. This enables all students in the class to see the steps within a strategy—steps they may not have been aware they were moving through.

Once the classroom discussion is complete, hang a poster of the various scribed strategies in a visible area so that students can return to it and use it to help solve other problems. When students have access to other students' thinking, their own repertoire of strategies will increase.

Games Using the Hundreds Chart

G-1	Number Chart Bingo!	97
G-2	Too High, Too Low	103
G-3	Fill It Up!	111
G-4	Mystery Squares	117
G-5	Don't Get Lost	123
G-6	Hippety Hop	133
G-7	Race to 100	142
G-8	101 and Out!	150
G-9	The Larger Difference	161
G-10	How Far Away?	173

Why these math games?

The games in this section provide excellent opportunities for students, working in pairs, to use a hundreds chart to reinforce concepts and skills introduced in the class lessons (L-1 through L-10). Games that are enjoyable for students are more likely to be played often, giving students the repeated experience they need with concepts like number comparisons, addition, subtraction, and place value. Repetition is important with games; each time students play, they benefit from the game in a slightly different way. The first couple of times when playing a game, the focus tends to be on the logistics (how to move, what to do on your turn, and so on). Subsequent plays allow students to interact with the game's concepts in a deeper way, focusing on the big ideas.

The first games in this section, *Number Chart Bingo!* (G-1); *Too High, Too Low* (G-2); *Fill It Up!* (G-3); and *Mystery Squares* (G-4) deal with foundational concepts such as identifying two-digit numbers, comparing numbers, and filling in missing numbers on a hundreds chart. *Don't Get Lost* (G-5) and *Hippety Hop* (G-6) give students practice with moving around on a hundreds chart. The last four games focus more specifically on learning place value and using a hundreds chart to add and subtract.

When should I teach with math games?

Finding time to give students repeated opportunities to play games can be challenging but rewarding. After you've taken time to introduce students to a particular game, have played the game during math time, and have had an opportunity to discuss the content and strategies, you can use that game repeatedly in stations, or centers, or when there is extra time during the day. This extra time might be in the mornings, when students are arriving and putting away their backpacks, during rainy-day recess, or during transition times (if there is time left during lunch or fine arts, for example).

Do I need to prepare materials in advance for these math games?

The Hundreds Chart

All the games in this section require the use of a hundreds chart or a portion of a hundreds chart. Sometimes we suggest you use a pocket hundreds chart with removable numbers. Other times, students will need their own copy of a hundreds chart, or you will want to have a paper copy or transparency to project (see the reproducibles). In our classrooms, we have a container (box or basket) that holds hundreds charts—copied on cardstock and laminated—for students to use any time they need one. We never make a fuss about which students need them and which do not; the charts are simply present at all times and are always available. In addition, we have students glue a copy of a hundreds chart on the inside front cover of their math journals. In this way, there is always a chart close at hand when students are working in their journals.

Counters

Several games require markers or counters. Small translucent-colored disks are the ideal counter to use in most hundreds chart games because the numbers on the chart show through. Other counters, such as pennies, can work as substitutes as long as the counter fits inside the numbered square (for more information about counters, see How to Use This Resource, page xix). If a game requires counters, ask students who come to the room early to begin counting out the needed supplies and to place them in containers or plastic sandwich bags. If you have enough materials, keep sets of twenty counters in plastic bags (snack-size freezer bags work best) at all times.

How do I manage my classroom during math games?

It's important to manage students during game play, and there are many techniques for doing so. It is your role, as the teacher, to set clear expectations and to supervise students while they are playing games. Many of the issues that arise when students are playing games can be avoided via careful preplanning. The following paragraphs provide a few helpful tips.

Assigning Partners

Assigning partners can be awkward for students, especially when they are assigned to play with someone whom they consider not to be a friend. Prepare students for assigned partners by setting clear expectations. Make it a goal from the beginning for students to have many different partners during the school year. State explicitly that it is inappropriate to show expressions of dismay or to say unkind words. Discuss disciplinary actions as necessary. In addition, let students know the length of time they will be expected to work with their partners, such as thirty minutes.

Letting Students Choose Partners

After the year is well under way and you have clearly established routines for playing games, consider allowing students to choose their partners. One structured way to start this process is to ask a few students as they arrive in the morning, "Whom would you like to play a game with during math?" Start a list of those who choose partners (and their corresponding partners). For those who do not choose a partner, assign them one and include them on the list. During math, read or post the list of partnerships without stating who picked their partners. This way, students won't feel like they were picked last.

In addition, when you give students the opportunity to choose partners, it's helpful to discuss with the class that sometimes best friends do not make the best game partners. Encouraging students to choose game partners with whom they work well helps students become responsible for their own learning. Once again, setting clear expectations is crucial; explain that if students choose someone and end up not following directions or not working well together, you will choose new partners for them.

Playing at Desks Versus the Floor

At the beginning of the year, as you are establishing routines for playing games, it is easier if students play all games at their desks. If they are using a single game board, such as a hundreds chart, ask them to sit next to their math partner so that the hundreds chart will be right-side up for both of them. If students are playing a game where they each have a hundreds chart, they still benefit from sitting side by side so they can clearly see the numbers their partner is marking. Many of these games require students to record something as they play. For this reason, working at desks may be preferable to sitting on the floor.

After routines are in place and students are demonstrating appropriate game-playing behavior, you might choose to move them to the floor. Students are more relaxed sitting on the floor, and materials may be easier for students to use when they are on the floor. When students play games on the floor, have them use clipboards or their math journals as "desks" for their worksheets while recording the results of their game. Sitting on the floor provides students with a more flexible seating arrangement, as well; they can sit either face to face or elbow to elbow. If students begin to act silly or are not following directions while playing on the floor, warn them that they will have to move back to their desks unless they behave appropriately. Be sure to follow through after your warning.

Managing the Use of Game Pieces

It's typical in any primary classroom to find game pieces left over on the floor from a previously played game. During the beginning of the year, explain your procedures for cleanup, including having students check around them, under them, and nearby for any stray materials. Be sure to allow ample time for students to practice these procedures early in the year while you monitor them, so that later in the year they will know your expectations for cleanup without your direct supervision.

Primary-age students are notorious for following teachers around the room, letting them know they found a counter, a tile, or a game marker. To help build autonomy, at the beginning of the year, hold up a found item then ask students to be problem solvers; encourage them to think quietly about where the item goes. Give students time to share their thoughts with their partners, then hold a class discussion about what to do when misplaced or lost items are found. This type of discussion encourages students to take ownership of their classroom and to put away these items on their own.

Keep in mind that for this approach to work, materials need to be readily accessible to students. Keep manipulatives in containers that are placed low enough for students to reach. Setting up a container or large plastic bag and labeling it *I'm lost!* for lost items helps students know what to do when they find a misplaced game piece but are unsure of where it belongs. At the end of the day or week, you can place these lost items in their proper place.

Why is it important to model math games?

For primary-age students, modeling how to play a math game is critical to the success they will have while playing it. We find it best to seat students on the floor while modeling a game. Have students sit on the perimeter of the whole-group area, and place the game materials in the center. This arrangement ensures that each student has a chance to see and hear what is going on while also being in close proximity to you. In addition, you can tell quickly who is and who is not paying attention, and can redirect behavior as necessary.

It helps to assign places for students to sit in the whole-group area; doing so alleviates students' desire to run to the front of the area or to save a seat for a friend. Also, consider placing students strategically who would benefit from sitting in the front of the group or closer to you.

There is more to modeling a game than simply explaining the instructions and walking through a pretend game. It's important to teach students explicitly the behavior you expect them to display while playing games in the classroom. For some students, this may be the first time they have played board or dice games and they may not know good game etiquette. Emphasize the following three behaviors when modeling: waiting patiently for your turn, passing game pieces to your partner appropriately, and winning or losing gracefully. It is also important for students to hear others' thinking about the game. While modeling the game, ask the key questions included with each game so that important mathematical ideas are discussed.

Modeling How to Wait Patiently for Your Turn

To model waiting patiently for your turn, remind students of what their role is while they wait. They might need to be checking their partner's work or checking their own work from previous rounds. Help them see that waiting is not a passive activity when playing math games, but is an active one. Let them know, however, that waiting patiently does not mean telling their partner repeatedly what to do or giving their partner the answer. Emphasize that such actions take the learning away from their partner. On the other hand, tell your students that if their partner asks for help, they may help.

Modeling How to Pass Game Pieces Appropriately to Your Partner

Passing dice or cards to a partner may seem trivial, but can turn quickly into an argument. Demonstrate for students how to wait politely for your partner to pass the dice when his turn is over, rather than grabbing them to begin your turn. Remind students that they should be watching their partner take a turn, and checking that they are following all the procedures of the game. Consistent teacher modeling of the appropriate way to pass game pieces will make this act second nature to students.

Modeling How to Win or Lose Gracefully

Learning how to win or lose gracefully is an important life skill for children. Whether playing math games at school or board games at home, students need to learn this skill, and modeling in the classroom is an important part of that learning. At the beginning of a game, explain that someone will win and someone will not win *this time*.

Explain to students that they have a choice about how to react at the end of a game. Whether they win or lose, their first statement should be, "Good game!" Remind them that everyone loses sometime and, although it is okay to feel disappointed, it is not okay to act out that disappointment with unkind words or actions. In the same way, nobody wants to play with someone who gloats at the end of a game they win. (*Gloat* might be a good vocabulary word to introduce!) Tell them that being a gracious winner or loser will ensure that friends will want to play the game with them again. **Note:** Having students play two against two can also help them feel more comfortable during competitive games.

What should I do while students are playing games?

While students are playing games, teachers should observe students, make note of what students write on their recording sheets, ask questions to extend students' learning and to assess their understanding, and work with small groups of students who need more help or when behavior issues or partner disputes arise.

Teaching Tip

Games Without Winners
Sometimes students have difficulty understanding that some games don't have a winner or loser. Games such as *Fill It Up!* (G-3) are played cooperatively, with the goal being to complete a particular task—in this case, filling an entire hundreds chart. Students take turns and work together to complete the chart. Be sure to explain that some games are played for the enjoyment of working together, and that during these games, both players are winners at the end.

Teaching Tip

Brainstorming How to Win or Lose Gracefully
Losing a game can seem like a big deal to a young child. It is helpful for them to have some words to say to express their feelings in an appropriate way. Hold a brainstorming session with your students about phrases they can say when they win or lose. Tell students that when they lose a game, they might say, "Oh, bummer. Maybe next time." Then ask students to think of other kind phrases they can say when a game is over. As students volunteer their thoughts, record the phrases on a poster or chart paper. Title the list, "What to Say When a Game Is Over" and post it on the classroom wall. As the year goes on, students can glance up to find words to say if they have trouble coming up with their own. During check-in discussions after games, ask students to report kind words they heard their partner say.

Using Recording Sheets

Recording sheets serve as both formative and summative assessments. Having students record their thinking while playing games is a valuable way to gain insight into students' understandings. Before introducing a recording sheet, make sure students are familiar with the game and have played it several times. Don't forget to model how to complete the recording sheet before handing it out to students. After students have started the game and are using their recording sheets, move around the room and note what students are writing. Ask students questions about what they have recorded. In addition, collect and review students' recording sheets to gain insight for planning next steps for the entire class or small groups of students.

Most teachers are required to indicate student understanding by assigning grades or checking off indicators. Recording sheets can serve as summative assessments when you need to assign a grade. Last, whether you use recording sheets to plan future lessons or indicate what has been learned, you'll find them helpful when discussing students' understandings with parents and administrators.

Number Chart Bingo!

Overview

In this lesson, the familiar game of *Bingo* is modified to create a tool that focuses on number sense, place value, and concepts such as even and odd. The game provides an opportunity for you to assess students' understanding of these concepts informally, as well. *Number Chart Bingo!* can be differentiated for kindergarten, or first or second grade by using different grade-appropriate *Bingo* clues.

Related Lessons

You might teach the following lessons first:

▶ L-5 One More or One Less

▶ L-6 Ten More or Ten Less

Consider this lesson as a follow-up:

▶ L-7 Hundreds Chart Riddles

Key Questions

▶ What were all the numbers that could have been marked for that clue?

▶ How did you decide which number to mark? (This question is for clues with more than one correct response.)

▶ Where did you find the number that was ten more than [number]?

Time

approximately 35 minutes

Materials

1–50 Chart (Reproducible B), 1 per student

counters, approximately 15 per student (see How to Use This Resource, page xix)

Number Chart Bingo! cards (Reproducible 15); 1 set, cut apart and assembled in a stack (for kindergarten, or first or second grade)

optional: *Number Chart Bingo!* Game Directions (Reproducible G-1R)

Time Saver

As students come to the classroom in the morning, have one or two students count sets of fifteen counters into resealable plastic bags.

Teaching Tip

Why a 1–50 Chart?
Although *Number Chart Bingo!* could be played on a hundreds chart with a modified set of clue cards, we suggest playing on a 1–50 chart for two reasons. The first is that when this game is played on a chart with one hundred numbers, it can take a very long time to get a Bingo. Young children are not known for their long attention spans and can become restless or lose focus in a lengthy game. The second reason is that some students can find a hundreds chart overwhelming as they search for the numbers that match the clues.

Technology Tip

Using an Interactive Whiteboard
If using an interactive whiteboard, have students come to the board and touch four numbers in a row horizontally, vertically, and diagonally to demonstrate how to get a Bingo.

Teaching Directions

1. Gather students together to introduce the game. Begin by asking, "Have you ever played *Bingo*?" Give students the opportunity to share what they know about the game of *Bingo*. Check that the main rules are covered:

   Main Rules of *Bingo*

   ▶ In *Bingo*, each player has a board with numbers on it.

   ▶ One person, the caller, calls out numbers.

   ▶ Players cover the number on their board, if they have it, with a counter.

   ▶ The game continues until one player has counters all the way across a row: horizontally, vertically, or diagonally and calls "Bingo!"

2. Explain that *Number Chart Bingo!* is similar to the game of *Bingo* in some ways. Each student will have a game board (a 1–50 chart) and counters.

3. Display a 1–50 chart so that the class can see it, either a large pocket chart with removable numbers, a chart projected with a document camera or overhead projector, or a chart on an interactive whiteboard.

4. Tell students that the object of the game is to get four counters on numbers that are next to each other, either vertically, horizontally, or diagonally.

5. Review the key vocabulary. Ask a student to come up and place four counters in a row, from side to side. Say to your students, "In mathematics, we call a line or row that goes from side to side a *horizontal* line." Ask students to repeat the word *horizontal* and to move their hands from side to side while saying the word. Repeat the process for the word *vertical*, having students make an

up-and-down motion while saying the word *vertical*. Because it is difficult to explain the position of counters placed *diagonally*, arrange four counters diagonally yourself, then give the students the word and have them repeat it as they move their hands *diagonally* in front of them. Show them that a Bingo can be achieved diagonally in two ways—from left to right and from right to left.

6. Next, tell students they will play one game together as a class before everybody gets a board of their own. Explain that the *Bingo* cards each have a clue to which number should be covered, and that there are two kinds of clues: open clues and closed clues. *Closed clues* are clues that have only one possible answer. For instance, if the clue says, *A number that is 1 more than 8*, there is only one possible answer. The only number that is one more than eight is nine. *Open clues* are clues that could have more than one answer. An example of an open clue is *An odd number that is less than 45*. Ask students, "Who can tell me a number that would fit this clue?" Ask several students to give examples of numbers that would fit the open clue, and emphasize that an open clue can have many answers. Make sure the students know that when they have an open clue, they can only cover one number, even though there is more than one answer.

7. Take the first card off the top of a stack of *Bingo* cards and read it.

8. Continue to play until there are four counters in a row horizontally, vertically, or diagonally. When this happens, tell students they can announce, "Bingo!"

9. Next, tell students that now that they have played *Number Chart Bingo!* as a class, they will now play it with their own card. Pass out the appropriate game boards (1–50 number charts) to students as well as sets of 15 counters enclosed in small plastic bags or other container.

Differentiating Your Instruction

Seeing and Hearing Key Vocabulary
English language learners as well as native English-speaking children benefit from learning mathematical vocabulary by seeing what the word means, then hearing the vocabulary, then using a body movement of some kind to reinforce the meaning of the concept.

Teaching Tip

Arranging the *Bingo* Card Stack
To familiarize your students with both kinds of clues, you can predetermine the arrangement of cards in your *Bingo* card stack. Ideally, the first card should be a closed clue, providing a clue to a single number on the board. The second card should be an open clue—a clue that could fit several numbers. For example:

> First Clue Card: *A number that is 4 tens and 6 ones.*

> Second Clue Card: *An odd number in the 30s.*

Technology Tip

Using a Document Camera
If you are using a document camera, display the card so students can see it as you read it.

ⓘ ## Teaching Tip

Discussing Multiple Numbers for Open Clue Cards
For the clues that have more than one correct answer (open clues), be sure to call on several students to explain which number they covered and why. At first, students may think the number they covered is the only possible answer, so it's important that they hear explanations about why other numbers fit open clues as well. Although more than one number may fit the clue, the rule is that only one number can be covered for every clue read.

10. Take one card off the top of the stack of clues and read it aloud.

11. After you read the clue, give students time to cover a number on their charts.

12. Ask a student to tell the class which number she covered and why. Then ask several other students to state which number they covered. Doing this allows students to confirm they covered the correct number; plus, students benefit from hearing the mathematical thinking of others.

13. Continue playing until one student calls "Bingo!" indicating she has four counters in a row on her board. (It's possible that two or more students could call "Bingo!" at the same time.)

14. Display the clue cards for the clues that have already been read. Have the student who called "Bingo!" tell the class which numbers she covered to make a Bingo (horizontally, vertically, or diagonally). For each number, ask the student to match one of the clue cards to it. If more than one student calls "Bingo!" at the same time, have them match their four covered numbers with the clues you have displayed.

A Child's Mind . . .

Which Clue Card Matches the Number?
Although it might be quicker to ask students to call out the numbers they marked and to verify yourself that the numbers match the clues you've read, it is important for the student to do the matching herself. This last step in the game provides another opportunity for the student to think about the clues and go through the mental process of deciding which clue matches which number. It is, in a way, a reversal of the original mental thought process the student went through to place the counter. Thinking about the numbers and their properties will strengthen students' number sense.

Time Saver

To shorten the game, change the goal so that students only have to get three counters in a row. Alternatively, to lengthen the game, change the goal so that students have to get five counters in a row.

Extend Their Learning!

Number Chart Bingo! is effective when played in small groups as well as in a whole-class setting. A teacher or instructional aide may use this game with a small group for extra support, or during an afterschool tutoring setting to reinforce number sense. If you are fortunate enough to have a parent volunteer in your classroom, this is a good game for volunteers to play with students. *Bingo* is usually familiar enough that a volunteer feels comfortable playing it with minimal direction from the teacher. Use Reproducible G-1R *Number Chart Bingo!* Game Directions as a quick-reference set of directions for school or home use.

Teacher Reflection

My Experiences with *Number Chart Bingo!*

Observing students play *Number Chart Bingo!* gives me the opportunity to assess students' number sense and mental arithmetic skills informally. Each time I call out a clue, I watch as students pause to consider the words and decide which number should be covered. Some students are quick to identify these numbers; they simply listen and respond immediately by placing a counter over a number. These students are able to calculate mentally ten more than or ten less than a number with ease. However, not all students are strong in auditory comprehension. Some students may need the support of seeing the card with the clue written. I display the clue using a document camera so that students who want to can read the words along with me. I also am careful to repeat the clue, giving every student the best opportunity to understand the clue.

I watch to see which students are thinking and using strategies when placing a counter for a clue that has more than one possible answer, and which students are placing counters more randomly. Recently, in a first-grade class, I observed Sarah and Joseph as they considered where to place a counter for the clue, *A number that is more than 30 and less than 39.* Sarah listened and found the row of thirties on her board. She smiled excitedly and placed her counter on number thirty-one. Joseph also found the correct row easily, but he took a bit of extra time and noticed that he had counters on forty-six and fifty-six already. He chose to place his counter on thirty-six, giving him three in a row. I made a mental note to keep an eye on Sarah, to determine whether she was using strategies and noticing other possible choices during the rest of the game.

Careful observation helps me notice how my students' number sense is progressing, as well. I watch when I call out a clue that has ten more or ten less in it. Do students find the number and just know to move down or up in the same column on the chart? Or do they count ten more or ten less to find the correct number to cover? The answers to these questions help me know from which games or activities these students will benefit in the future.

Too High, Too Low

Overview

During this game, students develop concepts of greater than and less than by trying to guess a mystery number. The hundreds chart serves as a map to keep track of their guesses and, ultimately, to reveal the mystery number. Consistent language and class discussions help students reflect on what they know about the mystery number and strategies for playing the game. There are two sets of directions—one for a whole-class game (to be played first) and one for a small-group game.

Related Lessons

You might teach the following lesson first:

▶ L-5 One More or One Less

Consider this lesson as a follow-up:

▶ L-7 Hundreds Chart Riddles

Key Questions

▶ What do you know about the mystery number?

▶ What is a helpful first guess and why?

ⓘ Teaching Tip

Alternatives to Red and Green Counters
If you do not have transparent red and green counters (color tiles or circles), use spray paint to cover lima beans in red and green. Another option is to laminate copies of The Hundreds Chart (Reproducible A) and give students red and green dry-erase markers.

Time

5 to 20 minutes

Materials

pocket hundreds chart with removable number cards *or*

hundreds chart projected on screen or interactive whiteboard

transparent squares in green and red (if using a pocket hundreds chart; see How to Use this Resource, page xviii)

game directions written on chart paper (for the small-group game)

The Hundreds Chart (Reproducible A), 1 per group

red and green counters, 1 of each color per group (see How to Use This Resource, page xix)

optional: *Too High, Too Low* Game Directions (Reproducible G-2R)

Technology Tip

Using an Interactive Whiteboard
If an interactive whiteboard is being used, simply highlight the guesses in green or red.

Differentiating Your Instruction

Ranges of Numbers
This game can be played with any range of numbers from one to one hundred. Kindergarten and first-grade classes generally benefit from using smaller ranges, like one to thirty, until they are comfortable with the phrases and the red and green markers. Most second-grade classes can begin by using the range one to one hundred.

Teaching Tip

The Importance of Consistency
During the game, keep the phrases consistent by always saying "Your guess is too high" or "Your guess is too low." Students can become confused if teachers change the phrases and begin saying things like "My number is higher than your guess," or various other statements to describe the guess and the mystery number's relationship to it.

Teaching Tip

Discussing the Mystery Number
It is not necessary to discuss what students know about the mystery number after each student is called on because this approach makes the game feel choppy, and students begin to lose interest.

Teaching Directions

Introduce: Whole-Class Game

1. Introduce the game. Let students know they will be working together to guess a mystery number. When they guess a number, you will tell them whether the guess is too high or too low. Tell them that if the guess is too low, you will place a green marker on the hundreds chart for the number that was guessed. If the guess is too high, you will place a red marker on the number guessed.

2. Begin the game by writing down the mystery number on a sticky note and keeping it hidden from students. Let students know they are welcome to begin guessing numbers from one to one hundred. Call on a student volunteer and, after the student has made a guess, reply by saying either: "Your guess is too high" or "Your guess is too low." Place the appropriate colored marker on the number guessed on the hundreds chart to indicate whether the guess was too high (red marker) or too low (green marker).

3. Call on another student to make a guess. After the student has made a guess, reply by saying either "Your guess is too high" or "Your guess is too low." Place the appropriate marker on the number guessed on the hundreds chart to indicate if the guess was too high (red marker) or too low (green marker). When a high number and a low number have been guessed, pause and ask students to think for a moment about what they know about the mystery number. After a few seconds, have students turn and talk with a partner about the mystery number.

4. Call on a few students to share what they know, then record their statements on chart paper.

Examples of Student Thinking and Teacher Recording

Example 1

Student says: "The mystery number is between forty-five and eighty."

Teacher records:

The mystery number is between 45 and 80.

45–80

As you record *45–80*, explain that this is a mathematical way to record the sentence that was just written. It can be read as "The mystery number is between forty-five and eighty."

Example 2

Student says: "The mystery number is higher than forty-five."

Teacher records:

The mystery number is higher than 45.

>45

As you record *>45*, explain that this is a mathematical way to record the sentence that was just written. It can be read as "The mystery number is higher than, or greater than, forty-five."

5. Continue to call on students to share their guesses. Pause after every couple of guesses to discuss and record what students know about the mystery number.

6. Continue playing the game until the mystery number is guessed. Remind the entire class that they worked *together* to guess the mystery number, rather than praising the individual student who guessed the mystery number. Confirm the mystery number by revealing your sticky note.

FIGURE G-2.1 JP guessed the number 45 and Mrs. Conklin placed the marker to highlight the number. She then gave a clue saying, "Your guess is too low."

Math Matters!

Connecting to Symbols
It may not be appropriate in kindergarten, depending on the state standards, to introduce and use mathematical symbols. Some begin using the symbols in first grade and continue in second grade. All grade levels benefit from seeing their thinking recorded in sentence form.

FIGURE G-2.2 After students talked with their discussion partner, Mrs. Conklin summarized what they already knew about the mystery number: it's between forty-five and eighty, and more than forty-five.

Explore: Small-Group Game

7. After students have played *Too High, Too Low* as a whole class, introduce the small-group game by reviewing the directions.

Too High, Too Low Game Directions

> ▶ The hider chooses a number, writes it down on a piece of paper, and keeps it hidden.

> ▶ The guessers take turns guessing numbers.

> ▶ After each turn, the hider uses the phrase, "Your guess is too high," and places a red counter or "Your guess is too low," and places a green counter.

> ▶ The hider uses red and green counters to mark the numbers guessed.

> ▶ When the number is guessed, the hider congratulates the group and shows the paper on which the number was written.

8. Hold up a copy of the hundreds chart and review how to mark the numbers that have been guessed using the green and red counters. Play part of a whole-class game to review the rules, using the key phrases, "Your guess is too high," and placing a red marker or "Your guess is too low," and placing a green marker. Remind students how to use the green and red markers.

9. Ask whether there are any questions. Explain how the groups will determine who will go first and so on. Sort students in groups of four and pass out a hundreds chart and one red counter and one green counter per group.

10. As students play the game, observe them in their groups and, periodically, ask the key questions listed at the beginning of this lesson.

Teaching Tip

Who Goes First?

So much time is lost in classrooms when students are trying to figure out who will go first (not to mention that unnecessary arguments can break out!). To deter this from happening, explain a method for determining who goes first before students are released to their groups. An easy way to determine an order is to have students go in alphabetical order by their first or last name.

Summarize: Whole-Class Discussion

11. When students have had several opportunities to play, hold a whole-class discussion. Ask students, "What is a helpful first guess and why?" Then ask, for example, "Why is fifty as a first guess more helpful than two?"

Extend Their Learning!

For homework, send materials and game directions (see Reproducible G-2R *Too High, Too Low*) home with a note attached asking parent and child to play the game three times.

Teacher Reflection

A Whole-Class Discussion on *Too High, Too Low*

After Ms. Hinkle's first graders had played *Too High, Too Low* several times, I gathered them together for a whole-class discussion. To start, I let them know what I was thinking:

"You've played *Too High, Too Low* a lot and I have been noticing some things about your guesses. I want to talk about which numbers are most helpful to use during your first guess and why." I then proceeded to ask, "Does anyone have ideas about helpful first guesses to make?" I paused and gave students time to think before calling on Elijah.

"I think twenty-two is a good first guess because it's my favorite number!" Elijah remarked. I resisted the urge to talk about why fifty would actually be a better guess than twenty-two. I knew Elijah would benefit more from a class discussion than from hearing me teach by telling. I wrote *22* where everyone could see it, then thanked Elijah for his thinking and called on Sophia.

"I think middle numbers are good," Sophia started to say, then walked to the hundreds chart and swept her hand across the forty and fifty rows. I asked her why and she continued, "Well, when you guess one of those numbers you know a lot and don't have as many numbers to work with."

I recorded *40–60* on the board and restated her thinking by saying, "Sophia believes forty to sixty are helpful guesses because you have fewer numbers left on the chart to worry about. Does anyone agree with her and would like to add on?"

Katie spoke up, "I agree because you knock off a lot of numbers. If I pick ten as my first guess then I know lots of numbers are left."

"It sounds like you are saying that if you guess ten and the guess is too low, then you have all these numbers to work with" (I pointed to 11 to 100), "but if you guess fifty and the guess is too low, then you only have these numbers to work with" (I pointed to 51 to 100). "Is that what you are saying?"

Katie enthusiastically confirmed, "Yes! You want to get rid of numbers so you find out the mystery number fast!"

"OK, any other ideas?" I queried. No one raised their hand. These students were still learning to talk about their thinking. I knew they would benefit from playing again and trying out strategies.

"I want you to play a few more times before we go to lunch. I would like you to use Elijah or Sophia and Katie's strategies. Either pick your favorite number like Elijah did or pick a number between forty and sixty and see which strategy helps you. Or you can make up a new strategy. We'll talk about this more another day."

I sent everyone off to play the game for the few minutes we had left before lunch. I planned on revisiting this discussion in a few days. I also looked for opportunities while students were playing to discuss their guesses with them. I've found that some of the best learning takes place when you can talk to a few students about a specific game they are playing, rather than when more general statements are made in a whole-class discussion.

Fill It Up!

Overview

During this game, pairs of students work together to fill a blank hundreds chart. They add or subtract numbers based on directions given on select *Fill It Up!* cards. The directions include cooperative and competitive versions of the game, as well as how to modify it for kindergarten. The game helps students construct a mental image of a hundreds chart, which is valuable as they begin to add and subtract larger numbers.

Related Lessons

You might teach the following lessons first:

▶ L-4 Building a Wacky Hundreds Chart
▶ L-2 Building the Hundreds Chart (Version 2)
▶ L-5 One More or One Less
▶ L-6 Ten More or Ten Less

Key Questions

▶ How can you quickly find the square when you need to subtract ____?
▶ How can you quickly find the square when you need to add ____?
▶ Your card says +/– ____. Which number will you subtract from or add to? Why?

Time

30 to 40 minutes (can be broken into two or more time periods)

Materials

1 blank 10-by-10 Grid (Reproducible D), either projected using a document camera, a transparency, or an interactive whiteboard

blank 10-by-10 grids, 1 per pair of students

Fill It Up! Cards, 1 set per pair of students (Reproducible 16)

2 number cubes, 1 set per pair of students

1 blank 10-by-5 Grid (Reproducible E) for the kindergarten version, 1 per pair of students

optional: *Fill It Up!* Game Directions (Reproducible G-3R)

Teaching Directions

Introduce

1. Gather students together to introduce the game. Project a blank hundreds chart (the 10-by-10 Grid, Reproducible D) using an overhead projector or document camera, or create a 10-by-10 grid on an interactive whiteboard.

2. Begin by writing the number *45* on the grid. Do a "think-aloud" as you decide where to place it. For example: "To find the right place for the number forty-five, I'm going to start with ten, because I know ten belongs in the square at the end of the first row, because every row has ten squares. Then I'm going to count down to see where forty would go." Count, "Ten, twenty, thirty, forty," as you move your hand down, indicating each row. "I know that forty-one will start the next row, so I count by ones from here— forty-one, forty-two, forty-three, forty-four, forty-five. So I know that this is the correct place for the number forty-five."

3. Explain to students that when it is their turn, they will choose a card with a direction for adding or subtracting one, two, ten, or twenty. They will decide which number to add to or subtract from each time.

4. Ask a student volunteer to come up and choose a card and read it to the class. If the card is labeled *+10,* ask students to think about what number is ten more than forty-five. Students may know that fifty-five is ten more than forty-five and then may be able to find quickly the correct square for fifty-five; some students may need to count on from forty-five to find the answer. They may choose to point to the squares as they count, so they find the spot for the number at the same time as they find the answer. When students have concluded that fifty-five is ten more than forty-five, write *55* in the correct location on the grid.

5. Now choose one of the –2 cards for modeling your next turn. Explain that students may play using the numbers forty-five or fifty-five. Ask students to talk to their math partner about what numbers are two less than forty-five and fifty-five. It's important for students to realize that there are now two possibilities: forty-three and fifty-three. Each choice made affects the choices that the next player has.

6. Depending on how students are responding, you may choose to continue playing the game until the end, or you may decide to send students off with partners to play the game independently.

Explore: Partner Game

7. To introduce the partner game, remind students of the directions. Tell them to take turns drawing one card and following the directions on the card to add to or subtract from a number on the grid. Explain that, near the end of the game, it is possible to draw a card for which there is no space to fill on the grid. If a player draws a card and cannot write a new number because it is already on the grid, the player should draw a new card. If, after four draws, a player cannot place a new number on the grid, the game is over.

Fill It Up! Game Directions

▶ Roll two number cubes and use them to make a two-digit number. Write that number where it belongs on the blank 10-by-10 grid. Check a completed hundreds chart to be sure the number you wrote is placed correctly.

▶ Mix up the *Fill It Up!* cards and place them face down in a pile.

Teaching Tip

Preparing a Blank Hundreds Chart (the 10-by-10 Grid)

There are a few options for preparing the materials for this game. You may choose to write in one number on the blank hundreds chart before making copies. If you do this, it's good to use a number about halfway between one and one hundred, so that there are many choices for students to write in numbers, and the board can grow in all four directions as they draw their first cards. Alternatively, copy the blank charts and let each pair of students fill in the first number. You might also choose for students to roll the number cubes to form a two-digit number as the beginning number for their chart.

▶ Take turns drawing one card from the pile and following the direction on the card to add or subtract from the numbers on the grid, then fill in the new number.

▶ If you draw a card and cannot write a new number because it is already on the grid, draw a new card. If, after four draws, you cannot place a new number, the game is over.

8. Pass out a 10-by-10 Grid (Reproducible D) and one set of *Fill It Up!* Cards (Reproducible 16) to each pair of students.

9. While students are playing *Fill It Up!*, ask the key questions listed at the beginning of this game. Observe students as they play and watch how they calculate to fill in the chart.

Summarize

10. After students have played several times, call them together to talk about the game. Begin with a simple question like, "What did you like about the game?"

11. Give students the opportunity to discuss their strategies for filling in numbers as well as any difficulties they may have encountered while playing the game.

ⓘ Teaching Tip

Filling in the Hundreds Chart
Observe students' strategies for how they calculate to fill the chart. If they are only counting by ones to subtract ten or twenty, it may be helpful to reteach L-2 *Building the Hundreds Chart (Version 2)* or L-3 *Arrow Arithmetic*.

Extend Their Learning!

Playing Competitively

Some students may enjoy playing competitively rather than cooperatively. The game can be adjusted easily for this by adding the following rule: Whichever card you draw *must* be played on the last number your partner wrote. For example, tell students that if their partner just wrote the number *15* and you draw a +2 card, they must write *17* even if there are other numbers on the grid to which they could add two. If they draw a card and can't write a number, they lose their turn. For example, if the game board looks like this:

	13	14	15	16	17			
				37				

and their partner just wrote *37*, if they draw the card −20 they would not be able to play and would lose a turn. The winner is the person who writes the last number on the grid.

Homework

For homework, send materials and game directions (see Reproducible G-3R *Fill It Up!* Game Directions) home with a note attached asking parent and child to play the game three times.

Modification

Kindergarten

Kindergarteners can play this game using a blank 10-by-5 Grid (Reproducible E) and a modified set of game cards (using just the +1, +2 and –1, –2 cards).

FIGURE G-3.1 Kindergartener Lawren draws a +1 card and records her answer on a blank 1–50 chart while her partner Katelyn watches.

FIGURE G-3.2 Near the end of the game, Katelyn adds one to forty-eight and records *49* on the 1–50 chart.

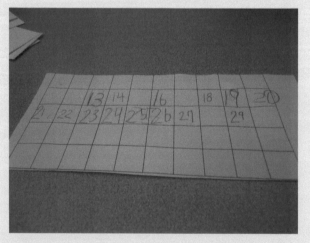

FIGURE G-3.3 The game began with 14 written on the blank 1–50 chart and Lawren and Katelyn drew cards to add or subtract 1 or 2 as the game progressed.

Mystery Squares

Overview

During this game, students are challenged to rely on their mental image of the hundreds chart (which previous lessons and games helped them construct) to identify numbers hidden (covered) by a mask. Several masks are provided so the teacher can differentiate the lesson for students at different grade levels as well as at different levels of proficiency with the hundreds chart.

Related Lessons

You might teach the following lessons first:

▶ L-1 Building the Hundreds Chart (Version 1)
▶ L-2 Building the Hundreds Chart (Version 2)

Consider these lessons as a follow-up:

▶ L-3 Arrow Arithmetic
▶ L-5 One More or One Less

Key Questions

▶ How did you know which number was hidden?
▶ Which direction is easier for you to work from to find the hidden numbers? From left to right or top to bottom? Why?

Time

25 to 35 minutes

Materials

The Hundreds Chart (Reproducible A) projected using a document camera, overhead projector, or interactive whiteboard

Mystery Squares Masks A and B (Reproducible 17), 1 each

optional: small white-erase boards and markers, 1 per pair of students

optional: *Mystery Squares* Masks: A and B (Reproducible 17), 1 per pair of students

optional: *Mystery Squares* Masks: C and D (Reproducible 17), 1 per pair of students

optional: *Mystery Squares* Game Directions (Reproducible G-4R)

Teaching Directions

Introduce

1. Gather students together and project the hundreds chart so everyone can see it.

2. After showing students the chart, take it away (or turn off the document camera or projector) and place Mask A (from Reproducible 17) on the chart so that numbers forty-two, forty-three, fifty-two, and fifty-three are covered.

3. Show the chart again and ask students to tell you what they notice.

   Examples of Student Thinking

   "Some of the numbers are missing."

   "You covered up part of the chart."

4. Ask students to turn to their discussion partner and tell him or her one of the numbers that is covered up, or missing.

5. Ask students, "Which number do you think is missing? How do you know?"

   Examples of Student Thinking

   "I think forty-two is missing because it should be right after forty-one."

   "I know forty-three is missing because it is ten more than thirty-three and so it goes under the thirty-three."

6. Model for students how to record a hidden number. Start by sketching the shape of Mask A. Draw a large square on a whiteboard or easel, then divide it in half vertically and in half horizontally so there are four boxes in which to write. Write a question mark in each box. As a student explains her thinking about a hidden number, be sure you know in which box the student thinks the number should be placed, then erase the question mark in that box and write in the number.

FIGURE G-4.1 Ms. Sullivan models for students how to record solutions for *Mystery Squares* by sketching a mask and filling it in. She is using a whiteboard for this purpose.

7. Continue having students explain, inviting them to come up and point to the numbers on the projected hundreds chart until all the missing numbers have been identified and written on the whiteboard.

FIGURE G-4.2 First grader Kayla explains how she solved *Mystery Squares*. She started at five and counted, saying, "Five, fifteen, twenty-five, thirty-five, forty-five, fifty-five." The Hundreds Chart is projected using a document camera.

8. For younger children, you may want to continue to use Mask A and repeat Steps 2 through 7, moving the mask to cover different numbers each time.

9. When students can tell you easily which numbers are missing, and explain their reasoning, place Mask B on the chart.

10. Ask students to tell their discussion partner one of the numbers that is hidden, and how they know. While they are talking, on the whiteboard draw another sketch in the shape of Mask B, with question marks in each square.

11. Ask students, "Which numbers do you think are hidden? How do you know?" After getting the first explanation, for example, "I know that sixty-five is hidden because I can see sixty-four and sixty-six, and sixty-five comes between those two numbers," ask students, "Is there another way to know that sixty-five is hidden?" This time a student might say, "I can see forty-five, and I know that twenty more than forty-five is sixty-five, so sixty-five has to be under the fifty-five."

12. Record students' thinking by erasing the appropriate question marks and writing in the hidden numbers on the sketched mask.

Explore

13. Explain to students that it's now their turn to play *Mystery Squares* with their partners. Give each pair of students a hundreds chart, a mask, and either a dry-erase board or their math journals.

Teaching Tip

Using All the Clues

Encourage students to use all the clues around the mask to help determine what is hidden. For instance, if you notice that students are justifying their answers primarily by adding one to the numbers they see, you might want to ask, "Can someone use one of the numbers below the mask to explain what the hidden number is?" or "Who can use this number [point to a number above the mask] to tell us what the hidden number below it is?"

Differentiating Your Instruction

Choosing the Mask

Reproducible 17 offers four mask options (A through D). Choose the mask you want your students to use by thinking about the responses students made during the first part of this game. If they were able to name the hidden numbers quickly and explain their reasoning accurately, you may want to give them Mask C or Mask D to challenge their thinking. Struggling students could continue to use Mask A or Mask B.

14. Direct students to take turns placing the mask on the chart while their partner hides his or her eyes.

FIGURE G-4.3 Emily decides where to place her mask on the hundreds chart while Asi'One looks the other way.

15. The second player then records the numbers he or she thinks are hidden, either by writing them on a small dry-erase board or in his or her math journal.

16. The first player removes the mask and both players check to determine whether the hidden numbers were recorded accurately.

FIGURE G-4.4 After Stephen recorded his solution, his partner Kayla revealed the mystery squares, and together they checked to be sure they matched. Stephen and Kayla are using laminated pieces of construction paper and dry-erase markers for recording as an alternative to commercially made white-erase boards.

Summarize

17. After students have had the opportunity to play a couple of times with one or two masks, gather them together to discuss their experience.

18. Use the key questions listed at the beginning of this lesson to encourage students to talk about their strategies for naming the hidden numbers.

19. Allow students to come forward and explain their reasoning using a projected hundreds chart.

Homework

Send home a hundreds chart, one or two of the masks, the game directions (see Reproducible G-4R *Mystery Squares*), and a note asking parent and child or older sibling and child to play the game. When students return to the classroom, give them an opportunity to share their homework experience with everyone.

Don't Get Lost

Overview

This game builds on students' prior experience with building hundreds charts and encourages them to create a mental image of a hundreds chart. Envisioning the charts helps students when they add and subtract numbers, and strengthens their concepts of the relative size of numbers less than one hundred.

Related Lessons

You might teach the following lessons first:

▶ L-1 Building the Hundreds Chart (Version 1)

▶ L-2 Building the Hundreds Chart (Version 2)

▶ L-4 Building a Wacky Hundreds Chart

▶ L-3 Arrow Arithmetic

Consider this lesson as a follow-up:

▶ L-6 Ten More or Ten Less

Key Questions

▶ What happens to the numbers as you move your finger down the chart in one column?

▶ What happens to the numbers as you move your finger from left to right? What about from right to left?

▶ What is a good strategy for finding your beginning spot on a blank chart?

▶ When is it better to start at the top of the chart and go down, and when is it better to move up from the bottom of the chart?

Time

20 minutes

Materials

blank hundreds charts, 1 per student (use the 10-by-10 Grid [Reproducible D])

completed hundreds charts, several available for the students (Reproducible A)

The Hundreds Chart (Reproducible A) projected using a document camera, overhead projector, or interactive whiteboard

counter, 1 per student

optional: *Don't Get Lost* Game Directions (Reproducible G-5R)

Teaching Tip

Small Groups

This game works best when played in a small group. Having just a few students around you will enable you to observe students closely and gives you the opportunity to check for accuracy as children move their finger on their chart.

Teaching Tip

Why a Blank Hundreds Chart?

Working with a blank hundreds chart helps students to create a mental map of the hundreds chart. They can use this mental map as they add and subtract numbers. It helps them develop a sense of where a number is on a scale of one to one hundred, and allows them to think flexibly about two-digit numbers.

Teaching Directions

Introduce

1. Gather a small group of students and pass out completed hundreds charts to each student. Begin by asking students to place their finger on number forty-three on the hundreds chart. Next, give a series of directions, one at a time, that allow students time to move their finger on their chart to match the directions. For example:

Directions Set 1

- ▶ *Start at 43.*
- ▶ *Move right 1 square.*
- ▶ *Move down 1 square.*
- ▶ *Move right 3 squares.*

2. Next ask, "What number are you touching now?" If all students did not end up on fifty-seven, repeat the directions, and follow them while pointing to a pocket hundreds chart or a hundreds chart on an overhead, document camera, or interactive whiteboard.

3. Show students a blank 10-by-10 Grid (Reproducible D) and ask them, "How is this like a hundreds chart? How is it different?" Pass out a grid and one small counter to each student. Allow students to count the rows and columns if they want to, to confirm that the chart is the same size as the hundreds charts they have been using.

4. Ask students to place their completed hundreds charts face down and to direct their attention to the blank hundreds chart. Begin by asking students to point to squares where familiar numbers would be if the chart were filled in. Start by asking them to put their counter on the square where number one would be, then one hundred, then ten.

Next, ask students to find the square where fifty would be and to place their counter on it. Have a student explain how he found the square for fifty.

Examples of Student Thinking

"I started at ten and counted down ten, twenty, thirty, forty, then fifty."

"I started at one hundred and I counted up—I mean back, like this: one hundred, ninety, eighty, seventy, sixty, fifty. So fifty is, like, here on this side, in the middle."

5. After you're sure students can find benchmark numbers, begin having them find the squares for other numbers on the chart. Each time they do this, have them explain how they knew the number would go there. Start with numbers that are close to benchmarks, like eight, thirteen, forty-eight, thirty, and ninety-seven, then move on to more difficult numbers, farther away from known benchmarks.

Explore

6. When students feel confident finding the place where numbers would be on a hundreds chart, you're ready to teach the game. Explain that you'll be giving them a series of directions, like you did in *Arrow Arithmetic* (L-3), but this time they place their counters on a *blank* hundreds chart and find where the numbers would be.

7. Begin by giving a short series of directions, such as the following:

Directions Set 2

▶ *Put your counter on 24.*

▶ *Move 1 space to the right.*

▶ *Move 1 space down.*

▶ *Where are you?*

Math Matters!

Counting by Ones
Don't be alarmed if a student starts with the first square and counts to twenty-four to find the beginning square. Many students go back to what they know when they are faced with something they perceive as new or "hard." Allow them to count to twenty-four, then encourage them to use their knowledge of tens and ones to find the twenty-fourth square. This teaching strategy will help them see they can trust using tens and ones without needing to count by ones each time.

8. Ask a student to demonstrate and explain how he moved his counter. Reread the directions slowly and have all the students in the group move their counters along with the student who is speaking.

9. Try more simple sets of directions, such as the following:

Directions Set 3

▶ *Find the square for 98.*

▶ *Move up 2 squares.*

▶ *Move left 1 square.*

▶ *Where are you?*

Directions Set 4

▶ *Find the square for 12.*

▶ *Move down 1 square.*

▶ *Move to the right 4 squares.*

▶ *Where are you?*

Directions Set 5

▶ *Find the square for 30.*

▶ *Move down 3 squares.*

▶ *Move to the left 2 squares.*

▶ *Where are you?*

10. As students gain confidence and are successful with easy directions, try more challenging sets of directions. Begin to ask the key questions listed at the beginning of this lesson.

Directions Set 6

- *Find the square for 24.*
- *Move down 3 squares.*
- *Move to the right 3 squares.*
- *Move up 1 square.*
- *Where are you?*

Directions Set 7

- *Find the square for 39.*
- *Move to the left 5 squares.*
- *Move down 3 squares.*
- *Where are you?*

11. After you teach this game to students in small groups, they may want to play in pairs on their own. Give one student a filled-in hundreds chart and her partner a blank chart and a small counter. Explain that the first student will give three or four directions while moving her finger on the hundreds chart. The second player should move his counter on the blank hundreds chart and tell his partner which number he lands on. Tell students they should talk and check their thinking after each move. Partners should switch roles after each round.

Example Partner Dialog

Student 1: "OK, start with your finger on the box for ten. Now move down two boxes."

Student 2: "Now I'm on thirty."

Student 1: " Move over one box to the left."

Student 2: "OK, that's twenty-nine."

Student 1: "Now go down one more box. Where are you?"

Student 2: "I'm on thirty-nine."

Student 1: "Yes! That's where I am too!"

Summarize

12. After students have played with partners, call the class together to discuss their experiences.

13. Use the key questions listed at the beginning of this lesson to encourage students to share their strategies.

14. Ask students to describe patterns or observations they noticed as they played, and record them where everyone can see them. If students have difficulty expressing generalizations, consider giving them a sentence starter such as, "When you move up a column on the hundreds chart . . . ," and then ask students to complete the sentence. This affords students one more opportunity to voice the patterns and structure that are inherent in the hundreds chart.

Homework

For homework, send materials and game directions (see Reproducible G5-R *Don't Get Lost*) home with a note attached asking the parent and child to play the game three times.

Teacher Reflection

My Experiences with Summarizing *Don't Get Lost*

After students had time to play with their partners, I called three pairs of students together for a brief discussion. Students were eager to share their experiences playing the game. I used the key questions as the basis of the discussion.

"I noticed that you all seemed to be moving around easily on your blank hundreds charts. What can you tell me about what happens as you move down the chart in a column?" I asked. I waited a few moments until several students had raised their hands and then called on Skylar.

"When you go down the chart, you get ten bigger each time," Skylar explained.

Bryce added, "Yeah, it's like the tens column goes ten, twenty, thirty, forty. All the other ones do the same thing, just their numbers are different."

"Do you mean all the other columns?" I clarified.

"Uh, huh," Bryce replied. "But if the column is, like, the five column, then all the numbers will end with five."

"Can anyone else point out on the hundreds chart the pattern that Bryce noticed?"

Andrew stood up and pointed to number 23. He said, "This one goes twenty-three, thirty-three, forty-three, fifty-three. All the numbers end with three because they're just ten more than the one on top of it."

I noticed that Andrew, Skylar, Alexa, and Rosa were nodding their heads in agreement. On the easel board in front of the group I wrote: *When you move down a column on the hundreds chart . . . ,* then asked, "Who can complete this sentence?"

Sebastian said, "The numbers get ten bigger." I was pleased to hear Sebastian's response because I wasn't sure of his understanding,

Math Matters!

The Importance of Repeated Experiences

Although students had previously made this observation in whole-group discussions, and we had recorded the ideas on the board, I took time to do it again. Students need repeated experiences with the same concepts to internalize ideas. These place-value concepts are vital to students' understanding of how our number system works, and for understanding concepts of addition and subtraction, so the time it took to restate them was not time lost.

and he was often hesitant to share aloud in our large-group discussions. Pulling him into a small-group discussion helped him feel more comfortable in sharing his thinking.

"Does everyone agree with Sebastian?" I asked.

Andrew responded, "It's like plus ten, plus ten, plus ten."

On the board I wrote +*10* next to the sentence. Then I asked, "What happens when you move up a space on the chart?"

"It's just the opposite," Rosa said. "It's minus ten, minus ten, minus ten." She went on, pointing to the numbers 65, 55, 45, and said, "The ones number stays the same and the tens number goes down one."

"Can anyone else say what Rosa was saying, but in your own words?" I asked.

Alexa raised her hand. "When you minus ten from a number, the number on this side stays the same," she said as she pointed to the 7s in the numbers 87, 77, 67, and 57. "The other numbers, like eighty, seventy, sixty, get ten less as you go up the column."

FIGURE G-5.1 Brayden and Skylar moved their counters to the correct square after hearing Ms. Sheffield say, "Move your counter to forty-five."

I restated what Alexa said. "So you're saying the number in the ones place stays the same and the number in the tens place decreases by ten when you move up the column?" Alexa smiled and nodded.

Next I asked, "Was there ever a time when you started at the bottom of your chart to find a space, rather than starting at the top?" Again I waited for at least half the group to raise their hands before calling on Andrew.

He answered, "If the beginning number is close to one hundred you can find it by going backward. Like one time Sebastian told me to find eighty-nine to start. So I started on one hundred, then went back one to ninety-nine, then up one to eighty-nine." As he explained, he pointed at the pocket hundreds chart.

Skylar added, "I would think about if the number was closer to one or closer to one hundred and then start with what it was closer to."

FIGURE G-5.2 Ms. Sheffield said, "Move your counter five squares to the right." Brayden knew he was on fifty by starting at ten and counting down the column by tens. Skylar knew she was on fifty by starting at forty-five and counting by ones to fifty.

"But if it's fifty-something it doesn't really matter cause it's in the middle," Sebastian pointed out.

This short conversation gave me a clear understanding of the strategic thinking this group was doing, as well as gave me the opportunity to revisit the important place-value ideas in the game.

FIGURE G-5.3 At the end of this round, Brayden's counter is on the fifty-eighth square, and he recorded where he landed by writing on the table with a dry-erase marker.

Hippety Hop

Overview

During this game, students use hops of one, ten, or one hundred to reach a target number on the hundreds chart. The goal is to reach the target number in the fewest hops. The game increases students' understanding of number relations and develops computational fluency.

Related Lessons

You might teach the following lessons first:

▶ L-1 Building the Hundreds Chart (Version 1)

▶ L-2 Building the Hundreds Chart (Version 2)

▶ L-6 Ten More or Ten Less

Consider this game as a follow-up:

▶ G-10 How Far Away?

Key Questions

▶ Why did you choose the set of hops that you did?

▶ Why might you sometimes go past the target number while hopping?

Time

30 to 45 minutes

Materials

pocket hundreds chart with removable number cards *or*

hundreds chart projected on screen or interactive whiteboard

The Hundreds Chart (Reproducible A), 1 per pair of students

sheets of paper, 1 per pair of students

optional: *Hippety Hop* Game Directions, Cooperative Group version (Reproducible G-6Ra)

optional: *Hippety Hop* Game Directions, Competitive version (Reproducible G-6Rb)

Teaching Directions

Introduce

1. Gather students where everyone can see a displayed hundreds chart. Explain *Hippety Hop* to the students. Tell them they will be given a target number to reach by making hops of one, ten, or one hundred. They may add or subtract to move to the target number. The object of the game is to get to the target number in the fewest hops.

2. Model one round for the students by writing the target number *18* for all to see. Explain the various ways to "hop" to 18:

   "I can hop to eighteen by making eighteen hops of one." Move your finger one number at a time from 1 to 18, then record *1 + 1 + 1 + 1 + 1 + 1 + 1 + 1 + 1 + 1 + 1 + 1 + 1 + 1 + 1 + 1 + 1 + 1.*

   "Or I can hop to eighteen by making some hops of tens and ones. I'll hop to ten and twenty, and then back two ones." Move your finger to 10, 20, 19, 18, and record *10 + 10 − 1 − 1 = 18.*

   "Or I can hop to eighteen by making a hop of ten and some hops of ones. I'll hop to ten and then make eight hops of one to eighteen." Move your finger to 10, 11, 12, 13, 14, 15, 16, 17, 18, and record *10 + 1 + 1 + 1 + 1 + 1 + 1 + 1 + 1 = 18.*

3. Emphasize to students that each number, whether it's a plus or a minus, represents a hop. Point to +10 and ask, "What does this plus ten represent?" Repeat this questioning procedure with +1 and −1.

   ### Examples of Student Thinking

   "That means you moved down to ten, then did it again from ten to twenty."

   "It means you added ten."

   "It means you moved your counter to ten."

A Child's Mind . . .

Making Connections
Don't assume that all your students understand that the equations you are writing represent the movement your finger makes on the chart. Be explicit about the connections and ask key questions to probe students' understanding of the representations. Some children are only able to focus on one action or the other and sometimes miss the connections.

4. Point to the first equation and ask the class to count the hops with you as you point to each +1. Record *18 hops* next to the equation. Point to the second equation and ask the class to count the hops with you as you point to 10 + 10 − 1 − 1. Record *4 hops* next to the equation. Point to the third equation and ask the class to count the hops with you as you point to 10 + 1 + 1 + 1 + 1 + 1 + 1 + 1 + 1. Record *9 hops* next to the equation. Ask, "Which equation gets us to our target number in the fewest hops?" Circle or star the correct equation.

5. Model another round with the students, but this time elicit their thinking. Write the target number *74* where everyone can see it. Tell the class you would like to start off by modeling one way to hop to seventy-four.

   "I'm going to hop to one hundred and back three tens to seventy, then forward four hops of one to seventy-four. Can someone revoice that as I record the equations?" Move your finger to 100, 90, 80, 70, 71, 72, 73, 74.

   As a student revoices your moves, record *100 − 10 − 10 − 10 + 1 + 1 + 1 + 1 = 74*.

6. Ask your students to think about how they would like to hop to seventy-four using one, ten, or one hundred. Give them a few moments to think, and then ask them to turn to their partner to explain how they would hop to seventy-four.

Teaching Tip

Revoicing

If students are new to being asked to revoice someone else's thinking, you may have to repeat your thinking a few times before a student is able to revoice it. The purpose of asking students to revoice is to give the class another opportunity to hear the same idea, therefore allowing for more processing time. To learn more about revoicing, we recommend reading *Classroom Discussions: Using Math Talk to Help Students Learn*, by Suzanne H. Chapin, Catherine O'Connor, and Nancy Canavan Anderson (Scholastic, 2009).

Differentiating Your Instruction

Allow students to have a hundreds chart in front of them so they can make hops to the target number independently before showing their thinking on the class hundreds chart.

Teaching Tip

Discussion Buddies

Oftentimes, students don't know who to turn to when teachers ask them to talk to a partner. To save time and alleviate any issues that might arise, assign "discussion buddies" before class discussions. Consider keeping the discussion buddies for several weeks so students become comfortable with their partner. Then switch buddies so students have opportunities to work with other classmates.

Teaching Tip

Recording Hops

If a student wants to make seventy-four hops of one, consider recording it as *1 + 1 + 1 + . . . 1 + 1 + 1 = 74* so the class does not become restless as you try to write *+1* seventy-four times!

Teaching Tip

Routines

This lesson works best if the introductory steps are used as a class routine several times before students play the game independently. Students benefit from class discussions and seeing the equations written during the introduction before they attempt to record equations on their own.

7. Call on a few students to explain how they would hop to seventy-four. Have them come up to the class hundreds chart to show their hops. When a student is finished, call on another student to revoice the hops. Record the hops using equations.

8. When a few equations have been recorded, ask the class to count the hops with you by counting the addends in each equation. Record the number of hops next to the equations and discuss which equation used the fewest hops. Circle or star the equation with the fewest hops.

Explore

9. Tell students they will work with a partner and hop to the target numbers, trying to make the fewest hops possible. Explain that, just like when you played the game together as a class, they will write the equations and then count the hops.

10. Model another round with the class and allow students to ask questions if they need clarification.

11. Pair up students and pass out one sheet of paper and one hundreds chart (Reproducible A) per pair. Record the following target numbers for all to see: *16, 33, 78, 82,* and *55.*

Differentiating Your Instruction

Working with Small Groups

If you believe a few students may struggle with this game, work with them in small groups. Model one way to hop to sixteen and ask a few of them to revoice what they heard. Give them their own hundreds chart and tell them to find another way to hop to sixteen. When they tell you their thinking, record the equations for them. Give each of them a piece of paper so they can practice writing equations, first copying what you did, then gradually writing equations on their own with your support.

12. Observe students as they work. Engage them in conversation and ask the key questions listed at the beginning of this game.

Summarize

13. Ask students to review their equations, then begin a class discussion to find the fewest hops for each number. Record only the equations with the fewest hops for each number.

    Ask, "When is it most helpful to hop to one hundred? Why? When is it most helpful to hop past the target number? Why?"

Teaching Tip

For Those Who Finish Early
If pairs finish early, allow them to choose their own target numbers and record their hops to that number.

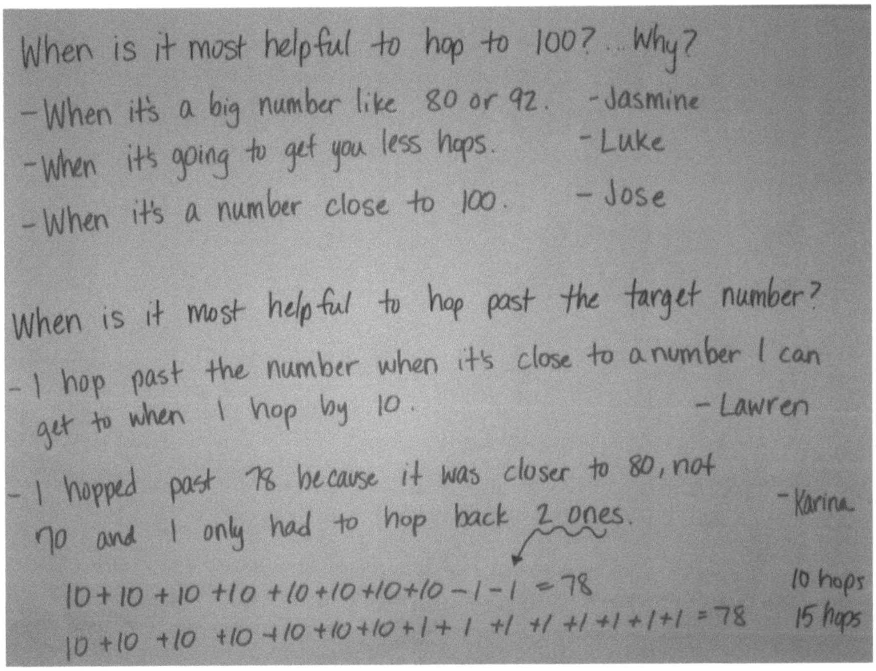

When is it most helpful to hop to 100?... Why?

- When it's a big number like 80 or 92. — Jasmine
- When it's going to get you less hops. — Luke
- When it's a number close to 100. — Jose

When is it most helpful to hop past the target number?

- I hop past the number when it's close to a number I can get to when I hop by 10. — Lawren

- I hopped past 78 because it was closer to 80, not 70 and I only had to hop back 2 ones. — Karina

$$10 + 10 + 10 + 10 + 10 + 10 + 10 + 10 - 1 - 1 = 78 \qquad 10 \text{ hops}$$
$$10 + 10 + 10 + 10 + 10 + 10 + 10 + 1 + 1 + 1 + 1 + 1 + 1 + 1 + 1 = 78 \qquad 15 \text{ hops}$$

FIGURE G-6.1 Mrs. Conklin's recording of students' answers to the key questions during the class discussion.

Extend Their Learning!

Competitive Version

Cut up a copy of The Hundreds Chart (Reproducible A) to form a stack of target number cards. Have students draw a number. This is their target number. Each student hops to their target number, records the equation, and counts the hops. The student with the fewest hops wins the round. Have students play five rounds. See *Hippety Hop* Game Directions, Competitive version (Reproducible G-6Rb).

Homework

Ask students to pick three target numbers or assign them three target numbers and have them play *Hippety Hop* at home (see Reproducible G-6Ra or G-6Rb).

Teacher Reflection

My Experiences Preparing Students for the Exploration Part of *Hippety Hop*

I want students to feel comfortable recording equations and counting hops before sending them to work with a partner. I normally use one target number a day as a routine to begin math class. This approach helps my students become comfortable with the game. Before starting the explore (partner work) part of the game, students have had multiple opportunities to come up to the class hundreds chart to make hops, watch me write equations, and count the hops as a class. On this particular day, I felt that the students were ready to move on to the exploration part.

I started by saying, "Today you will work with a partner and record your own equations for *Hippety Hop*. I want to make sure you are comfortable doing this on your own, so please ask questions if you have them. Let's do one together. Our target number will be sixty-four. Think quietly for a moment about how you would hop to sixty-four. I've placed hundreds charts on the carpet for you to use, or you can look at the pockets hundreds chart."

I paused for several moments as students worked to hop to sixty-four. I noticed that most of the students were referring to hundreds charts I had placed on the floor. I could see them using their fingers to make hops, and counting the hops as they went. One student asked if he could get some paper to write the equations because he couldn't keep up with his hops. Of course I allowed him to get paper. A few students, mainly those in the front row of the whole-group area, were using the class pocket chart.

"I would like for you to turn to your discussion buddy and explain how you would hop to sixty-four," I said. Then I got up so I could move around the groups and listen to students' conversations. I did this so I knew on whom to call for the class discussion. I listened for differing strategies on how to hop to sixty-four so we had a variety of equations to discuss. I also made mental notes about who was struggling with this concept so I could meet with them in a small group at a later time, or check in with them during the exploration.

When students were ready, I called on DeTron to explain how he would hop to sixty-four. DeTron eagerly approached the pocket hundreds chart and began to explain his thinking.

"I would hop like this: ten, twenty, thirty, forty, fifty, sixty, sixty-one, sixty-two, sixty-three, sixty-four," DeTron gestured.

I asked, "How many hops did you make?"

DeTron repeated his movement, this time counting his hops. "Ten hops to get to sixty-four," he declared.

"OK, thanks DeTron. Did DeTron hop by ones, tens, or hundreds first?" I asked the class. The overwhelming answer was "By tens!"

"So we are first going to start our equation with ten," I said, writing the number *10* on chart paper. "DeTron, show us what you did next, please?"

DeTron showed the class, explaining, "I added more tens until I got to sixty."

"So what should we write to match DeTron's thinking?" I asked. Students began talking to their discussion buddies about what to write. I quieted the class down and called on Kylie.

"You should write ten plus ten plus ten plus ten plus ten plus ten, because DeTron made six jumps of ten." Kylie explained.

I saw that most of the students were nodding in agreement. I recorded what Kylie said and then asked DeTron to show us what he did next. He told the class about making four hops of one. Again, I asked the class to think about what we should write to show DeTron's thinking.

I called on Nico, who stated, "You should write plus one four times since he made four hops of one. One plus one plus one plus one, and then write equals sixty-four."

I recorded what Nico said and asked the class to look at the equation and count the hops with their discussion buddy. I reminded them that DeTron said he made ten hops, and asked if they agreed. They all agreed. I called on two more students to share how they hopped to sixty-four. I repeated the same procedure by asking the students to make the hops, and then engaged the class in a discussion on how to write the equations.

"Today, you will work with a partner and make hops to the target numbers I assign you. On your paper you will write the various ways you hopped to the target number. Remember to count the hops and record that, too. You are trying to make the fewest hops, so when you think you have reached the target number in the fewest hops, you can go on to the next target number."

"Do we both record the number sentence?" Lawon asked.

"Great question, Lawon. No, I'm giving you one sheet of paper and one hundreds chart. I am hoping you will work together with your partner. This means you need to talk to your partner and work together to agree on the way the number sentence should be written, and if you think you made the fewest hops to the target number." I clarified.

"Can I pick my partner?" Jessica queried.

"I am going to pick your partner today. I want to remind you that when I pick your partner, there is an appropriate way to react and I expect you to react that way. Remember, no moaning or rude looks. We need to learn to work with everyone in the class. Do you all understand what I expect of you?" The students nodded. We had recently had some minor issues with certain students who wanted to work with their best friend and who did not react appropriately when assigned to work with another student. After this happened, we held a class meeting about how to react when a partner is assigned to you.

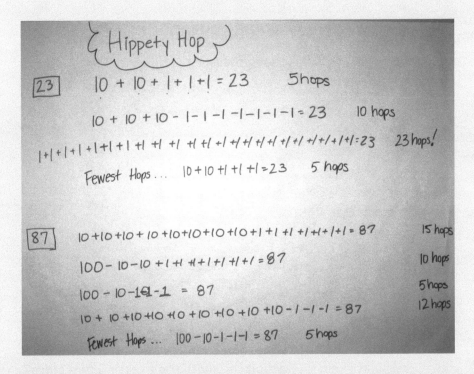

FIGURE G-6.2 Mrs. Conklin's recording of equations to match the hops students made to reach the target numbers twenty-three and eighty-seven.

Game 7

Race to 100

Time

45 to 60 minutes

Materials

The Hundreds Chart (Reproducible A), 1 copy per player

Race to 100: Fives Strips (Reproducible 18)

Race to 100: Tens Strips (Reproducible 19)

Race to 100: Action Cards (Reproducible 20)

Race to 100: Question Cards (Reproducible 21)

optional: *Race to 100* Game Directions (Reproducible G-7R)

Overview

During this game, students add or subtract five, ten, or multiples of ten as they try to reach or go over one hundred before their partner. During each turn, students answer a question that gives them an opportunity to think more about number relationships, and to practice adding or subtracting. Two options for class discussions provide you with a chance to discuss linking student thinking to symbols or linking student thinking to the various ways to decompose a number.

Related Lessons

You might teach the following lessons first:

▶ L-2 Building the Hundreds Chart (Version 2)

▶ L-3 Arrow Arithmetic

▶ L-6 Ten More or Ten Less

Consider this game as a follow-up:

▶ G-8 101 and Out!

Key Questions

▶ How did you solve what was asked of you on the action card?

▶ How did you solve what was asked of you on the question card?

▶ How can you make the number on the action card with the fives and tens strips?

Time Saver

Preparing the Cards

Copy the action cards and question cards on different-color paper so they can be sorted easily, shuffled, and placed into two piles.

Teaching Directions

Introduce

1. Gather students in a circle and place the materials in the middle of the circle so all students can see them.

2. Tell students they are going to learn to play *Race to 100*. The objective of the game is to get to or go over one hundred before your opponent. To play, you draw an action card, perform the action by placing the appropriate strips on a hundreds chart, then draw a question card and answer the question. Play continues until someone gets to or goes over one hundred.

3. Model for students how to shuffle the action cards and place them in a pile. Do the same with the question cards and place them in another pile.

4. Select a student to play against you. Place a hundreds chart in front of the student and one in front of you. Place the fives and tens strips in the middle so that you can both reach them. Explain to students they will draw an action card and find the appropriate strips to place on the hundreds chart. If they draw a minus card in the first round, they need to place it in the middle of the action card pile and draw again. Model the first round for them. The following is a sample teacher explanation: "I drew a plus-twenty action card from the pile. This means I need to add twenty, or cover twenty spaces on the hundreds chart. I can make twenty using two tens strips because ten plus ten is twenty. I could also use four fives strips because five plus five plus five plus five is twenty. I'm going to choose to cover twenty spaces with two tens strips."

5. Next, draw a question card and read the card aloud to the class. The question card is: *What is 10 more than what you have right*

Teaching Tip

Shuffling Cards
Show students how to shuffle the cards quickly by turning them face down and swirling them around. This is much easier for students than trying to shuffle the cards the traditional way.

A Child's Mind . . .

Help Me Think

Many students, when playing math games, do not realize they are engaging in math and may not think deeply about the math in which they are engaging. In *Race to 100*, the purpose of the question cards is to help students pause briefly and think more about the game they are playing. The question cards help children think about number relationships and basic addition or subtraction.

now? Pause for a few moments to give students time to think about the answer. Ask them to whisper the answer to a partner and then raise their hand if they are willing to share their thinking.

Example of Students' Thinking

"I put my finger on twenty and counted ten more. I landed on thirty."

"I know that twenty plus ten is thirty."

"I know the number under twenty on the hundreds chart is ten more. It's thirty."

6. After you have completed your round with the student, model placing the action card into one discard pile and the question card into another discard pile. Ask the student to go next.

7. For your next turn, tell the class you are going to find, purposefully, the −5 action card so they can have a discussion.

8. Point to the two tens strips and explain that you will need to trade for some fives strips because you don't have a fives strip to take away. Pick up one tens strip, lay it to the side, and then place two fives strips under it so students can see they are equal. Explain the trade to students before putting the two fives strips on the hundreds chart.

9. Next, remind students that they need to take five away (per the action card). Pick up the fives strip from the hundreds chart. Ask students, "What is twenty minus five?"

A Child's Mind . . .

Finding Shortcuts

At first, students may need to trade by laying strips underneath each other so they can see they are equal, then use the appropriate strip. After several turns or games, students may find shortcuts. Encourage this!

10. Then, draw a question card and read the card aloud to the class. The question card is: *How many more do you need to reach 100?* Pause for a few moments to give students time to think about the answer. Ask them to whisper the answer to a partner and then raise their hand if they are willing to share their thinking.

Examples of Students' Thinking

"I added five to get to twenty and counted by tens to one hundred. It was eighty, and eighty plus five is eighty-five."

"I put my finger on fifteen and counted by tens to ninety-five. It was eighty. I counted five more to get to one hundred; eighty plus five equals eighty-five."

11. Finish a complete game with students so game scenarios can be discussed before students play with a partner.

Explore

12. Put students into pairs. Give each pair two hundreds charts, a set of action and question cards, and fives and tens strips. You may also want to give them a copy of the game directions as a reminder (see Reproducible G-7R).

13. Observe as partners play. Assist when needed, and ask the key questions listed at the beginning of this game.

Teaching Tip

Working with Small Groups
As an alternative to playing with partners, consider playing the game with small groups of students until they are comfortable enough to play without assistance.

Differentiating Your Instruction

Omitting or Modifying the Question Cards
You may decide some partners would benefit from playing the game without the question cards. The purpose for playing without the question cards is to give students more time to focus on computation while learning the game. Alternatively, you may choose to modify the questions to suit the students' level of learning more completely. You may opt to use only one question, such as: *How many more do I need to reach 100?* Some learners would benefit from working on the missing addend. Or you may choose to use the questions about adding five or ten more to the number, for those learners who would benefit from working on mental math.

Teaching Tip

Discussion Buddies

Oftentimes, students don't know to whom to turn when teachers ask them to talk to a partner. To save time and alleviate any issues that might arise, assign "discussion buddies" before class discussions. Consider keeping the discussion buddies for several weeks so students become comfortable with their partner. Then switch buddies so students have opportunities to work with other classmates.

A Child's Mind . . .

Making Individual Hundreds Charts Available

Many students will need their own hundreds chart to figure out the difference between forty-five and one hundred. Have several hundreds charts available for students to use.

Class Discussion: Option 1

1. After students have had time to play the game, begin a class discussion with the purpose of linking their thinking to the symbols.

2. Display a hundreds chart with forty-five spaces covered. Ask the following question from the question card pile: "How many more do you need to reach one hundred?" Ask students to think quietly for a moment about the question and then share their thoughts with a partner.

3. Call on a few students to share their thinking. Record their thinking symbolically.

    Example of Student Thinking and Teacher Recording

    Student 1 responds, "I put my finger on forty-five and counted by tens to ninety-five, then I counted by ones over to one hundred. So I said ten, twenty, thirty, forty, fifty, fifty-one, fifty-two, fifty-three, fifty-four, fifty-five. I know I need fifty-five to reach one hundred."

    Teacher records,

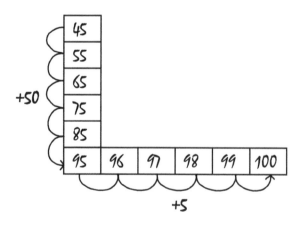

    Teacher says, "I drew a partial hundreds chart to show what you did. Another way we can record your thinking is with an equation. You said you started on forty-five and added fifty, so I'll record forty-five plus fifty equals ninety-five. Then you said you added five more, so I'll record ninety-five plus five equals one hundred. You looked at what you added and it was fifty-five."

$$45 + \boxed{50} = 95$$
$$95 + \boxed{5} = 100$$

$$55$$

Student 2 responds, "I did it in my brain. I counted to ninety-five. I said fifty-five, sixty-five, seventy-five, eighty-five, ninety-five, and saw I had five fingers up and that's fifty since I was counting by tens. Then I knew I needed five more to get to one hundred; fifty and five is fifty-five."

Teacher records,

Teacher says, "You used your fingers to keep track of your counting, which is helpful. We can also record your thinking with an equation."

$$45 + \boxed{50} = 95$$
$$95 + \boxed{5} = 100$$

$$55$$

4. Acknowledge the different ways of thinking about the same problem. Ask students to look for similarities in the different methods. Also, discuss the various ways to record student thinking.

5. If students are restless, end the class discussion for the day. Continue on another day with various other scenarios.

Class Discussion: Option 2

1. After students have had time to play the game, begin a class discussion with the purpose of linking to the various ways to decompose a number.

2. Display the action card +20 and ask students to think quietly for a few moments about the different ways they could create twenty using the tens and fives strips. Then ask them to turn and talk to their partner.

3. Call on a few students to share their thinking. Have them come up and display the tens and fives strips they would use to create twenty. Link their thinking to the equations.

Linking Thinking and Equations

Student says, "I made twenty using two tens strips."

Teacher records, *20 = 10 + 10*

Student says, "I made twenty using a fives strip a tens strip and another fives strip.

Teacher records, *20 = 5 + 10 + 5*

Student says, "I made twenty using a tens strip and two fives strips."

Teacher records, *20 = 10 + 5 + 5*

4. Display the question card, *How many ways can you make 30 using the fives and tens strips?* Ask students to think quietly for a moment and then have them go back to their seat to record their thinking. Let students know they may use equations or pictures to record the different ways to make thirty.

5. Continue on another day with various other scenarios.

Math Matters!

The Commutative Property

Students will typically offer the same numbers but in a different order. For example, 10 + 5 + 5 may already be displayed and a student will say 5 + 10 + 5. Allow this student to use the strips and record his thinking using an equation. Then ask the class if they can find an equation that uses the same numbers. Explain that when we add, we can put numbers in any order and still have the same sum. Your students have just discovered the commutative property!

Homework

For homework send home the same question (*How many ways can you make 30 using the fives and tens strips?*), but use the number forty-five or fifty.

Teacher Reflection

Recording Student Thinking: Class Discussions

Recording student thinking has helped me get to know my students better and has helped my students be able to record their thinking. However, when I ask students to record their thinking, they sometimes seem confused about what to write on their paper. I've found that holding class discussions during which students explain their thinking as I act as their scribe helps them learn how to record their thinking independently. (It also takes less time if I do the recording, which is important when you have more than twenty primary students sitting in a whole-group area!) These discussions benefit everyone; students hear how one of their peers solved the problem, and they see what the solution looks like on paper. Drawings of a partial hundreds chart, open number line, or an illustration of hands (if the student counted on her fingers) are all direct representations of how students may think through a problem to the solution. I aim to honor students' way of thinking while also linking their thinking to more abstract symbolism such as equations or number sentences.

During a class discussion, I often choose to call on two or three students who I have been observing while they played the game. I want a variety of solution strategies shared, so students can evaluate which strategy matches most closely how they solved the problem, and so students can see that there are many efficient ways to solve (and record) the same problem. Last but not least, as I record, I make sure to pause and to ask clarifying questions.

Game 8

101 and Out!

Time

45 to 60 minutes

Materials

The Hundreds Chart, 1 per student (Reproducible A)

pocket hundreds chart with removable numbers *or*

hundreds chart projected on a screen or an interactive whiteboard

101–200 Chart, 5 or 6 per class (Reproducible C)

dice, 1 per pair of students

counters, 1 per student

101 and Out! Recording Sheet, 1 per student (Reproducible 22)

101 and Out! Assessment Sheet, 1 per student (Reproducible 23)

optional: *101 and Out!* Game Directions (Reproducible G-8R)

Overview

This game involves addition as well as place value. It gives students an opportunity to think strategically while working with the concepts of ones and tens. Class discussions and opportunities to write about their thinking help students develop more effective strategies.

Related Lessons

You might teach the following lesson and games first:

▶ L-6 Ten More or Ten Less

▶ G-7 Race to 100

▶ G-10 How Far Away?

Key Questions

▶ Will you place the number in the ones place or the tens place? Why?

▶ What do you hope to roll next? Why?

▶ If you rolled a 2 on your first roll, where might you place it and why?

Teaching Directions

1. Gather students together and introduce *101 and Out!* Explain to students they will roll a die, decide whether the number should be placed in the ones place or the tens place, and repeat this five more times, adding the numbers each time. The objective is to try to get as close to one hundred as you can without going over.

2. Call on a student to play with you and display two hundreds charts, one for you and one for the student.

3. Model rolling the die. Place a counter on the number you rolled on the hundreds chart. Record the number on the recording sheet. Share your thinking aloud to help students understand the concept of the game. For example, "I rolled a five. I can place the five in the ones place so the value is five, or I can place the five in the tens place so the value is fifty. I'm going to put it in the tens place to create the number fifty. I made it fifty instead of five because I want to try to get close to one hundred and I have five more rolls left. I can put the numbers for my other rolls in the ones place so that I don't go over one hundred. I'm going to move my marker to fifty and record fifty on the recording sheet."

4. Pass the die and ask the student volunteer to roll it. Talk with the class about the two numbers that can be created by putting the number in the ones place or the tens place. Ask the student volunteer, "Which number would you like to create?" Have the volunteer place the counter on the number she chose on the second hundreds chart.

Technology Tip

Using an Interactive Whiteboard
If an interactive whiteboard is being used, project two hundreds charts side by side, one for you and one for the student volunteer.

Technology Tip

Using an Interactive Whiteboard
If an interactive whiteboard is being used, highlight the number fifty.

Teaching Tip

Should Strategies Be Discussed?
We recommend that you do not spend a lot of time explaining strategy to students. Students need several experiences of playing the game before they are ready to discuss a strategy.

Technology Tip

Using an Interactive Whiteboard
If an interactive whiteboard is being used, have the student volunteer highlight the number she chose.

5. Ask the student volunteer to pass the die back to you, and then you roll again. Again, model thinking aloud with students. Tell them the two numbers that could be created and use the hundreds chart to model adding those numbers to the previous round's number. Share which number you will use and why. For example: "This time I rolled a six and I can create a six or sixty. If I put my finger on the fifty from the last round and add six, I land on fifty-six. If I put my finger on fifty and add sixty, I'm off the hundreds chart. Since I know I have four rolls left and I want to be close to one hundred without going over, I definitely don't want to use sixty as my number. I would have too much! I'll use six and move my counter to fifty-six. I also have to remember to write down six on my recording sheet and find my total."

6. Pass the die to the student volunteer and model thinking aloud with the class once again, after the die has been rolled.

7. Roll the die for the third round. This time elicit student thinking. Ask students to turn to their partner and decide whether they would place the number in the ones place or the tens place. Encourage them to share with their partner why they made that decision.

8. Call on a few students to share their thinking. Use the hundreds chart to add the number rolled so students can see the two outcomes. Decide which number you will use, add it on the hundreds chart, and record it on the recording sheet. Pass the die to the student volunteer so she can complete her turn.

Teaching Tip

Discussion Buddies

Oftentimes, students don't know to whom to turn when teachers ask them to talk to a partner. To save time and alleviate any issues that might arise, assign "discussion buddies" before class discussions. Consider keeping the discussion buddies for several weeks so students become comfortable with their partner. Then switch buddies so students have opportunities to work with other classmates.

Time Saver

Balancing Discussion Time During Modeling

We recommend that you do not spend a lot of time talking about the student volunteer's turn with the class. Students become restless when they sit for too long. It is important to find the balance between meaningful class discussions that will help students be successful when they play the game, and class discussions that are too long and impede students' learning.

9. Continue for three more rounds. It may be necessary to use the 101–200 Chart (Reproducible C) if you or the student volunteer go over one hundred. To introduce the 101–200 Chart, place it directly below the hundreds chart and use the game counter to add the number rolled.

10. When the game is over (after six rounds), point to the hundreds charts or the recording sheet (Reproducible 22) and ask students to figure out which game is closest to one hundred without going over. Encourage them to talk to their partner about their thinking.

11. Call on a few students to share their thinking. Look for opportunities to use the word *difference* when students talk about how far from one hundred a player's total is.

Explore

12. Now it's the students' turn to play the game in small groups. Remind students of the game's rules: They roll one die, put the number in the ones or tens place, place their counter on the hundreds chart, and record on the recording sheet.

Game Directions

1. Roll the die.

2. Create a number.

3. Move your counter on the hundreds chart.

4. Record on the recording sheet.

5. Find the sum.

6. Pass the die to your partner.

Teaching Tip

Modeling
During the game's introduction, the first two rounds of play are used to model the decisions that must be made during the game, whereas the last four rounds engage students in thinking about the decisions. This number of rounds will prepare students to play on their own.

A Child's Mind . . .

Going over One Hundred
Don't be surprised if students go over one hundred the first several times they play the game. Students need repeated opportunities to learn about magnitude of numbers and number relationships. When students have rolled a number, engage them in a conversation to discuss the two outcomes: What will happen if they place the digit in the ones place? The tens place? These conversations help students begin to think strategically about the game.

Teaching Tip

Posting the Directions
Posting directions for everyone to see can be helpful for students who are playing the game for the first time. Directions do not have to be detailed. Short, concise phrases help students recall what they should be doing.

Teaching Tip

Managing the Use of Dice
Using dice can be problematic if students are rolling them across the entire floor or throwing them across a table. To prevent such scenarios, give each group of students a 6-by-6-inch square of soft foam or cotton batting, then tell students they will lose their turn if they roll the die off the foam. Setting such parameters decreases chaos (rolling—and in some cases, flying!—dice) and maintains control in the classroom.

Differentiating Your Instruction

Playing in Partners

This game requires students to have a good grasp of magnitude of numbers. Some students realize quickly that putting the number rolled in the tens place creates larger totals whereas other students need more time to develop this understanding. Students may be more successful at getting close to one hundred without going over if they play with a partner with whom they can discuss their decisions. If you choose to have students play with a partner, then during the introduction to the game you should also play with a partner, so you can model talking to your partner about the choices that arise during the game.

Technology Tip

Using an Interactive Whiteboard

If an interactive whiteboard is being used, highlight the number fifty-five and use the interactive pen to create the partially played game record shown here.

13. Distribute one recording sheet (Reproducible 22) and one hundreds chart (Reproducible A) per student, one die per pair of students, and two counters per pair of students. As students work on the activity, walk from group to group, asking the key questions listed at the beginning of this game.

Summarize

14. Ask students to return all the materials except the hundreds chart before beginning a whole-class discussion. Gather students together, letting them know they may use their chart during the discussion.

15. Display the following partially played game. Place a counter on the number fifty-five on a class hundreds chart.

Game 1		
Round 1		20
Round 2	+	5
Total		25
Round 3	+	30
Total		55
Round 4	+	
Total		
Round 5	+	
Total		
Round 6	+	
Total		

16. Tell students that the next number rolled is a 3. Ask them first to think and then to discuss with a partner what they would do. Would they put the 3 in the ones place or the tens place and why?

17. After students have had a few moments to think and talk, call on several students to share their thinking. Come to a final class agreement, move the counter on the hundreds chart, and record in Round 4 on the partially played recording sheet.

18. Tell students the next number rolled is a 1. Again, ask them first to think and then to discuss with a partner what they would do. Would they put the 1 in the ones or tens place and why?

19. After students have had a few moments to think and talk, call on several students to share their thinking. Come to a final class agreement, move the counter on the hundreds chart, and record in Round 5 on the partially played recording sheet.

20. Ask students to think quietly to themselves about which number they would hope to roll next. After they have had some time to think, tell them to turn and share their thinking with their partner. Call on a few volunteers to discuss their thinking.

Technology Tip

Using an Interactive Whiteboard
If an interactive whiteboard is being used, have a student volunteer highlight the partial sum to which the class agrees.

Teaching Tip

Writing in Math Class
Asking students to discuss which number they would like to roll next is a thought-provoking writing prompt. If students are new to writing about their thinking, it is helpful to facilitate a class discussion first, then release them to their seats to write. On another day, a new game scenario can be used, this time allowing students to write independently, without a class discussion to help them.

Extend Their Learning!

Play using a ten-sided, zero-to-nine die. Explain that if you roll a 0, you can roll again until you get a number that is one through nine.

Homework

Ask students to play the game three times and return the recording sheet for *101 and Out!* (Reproducible 22) to the class. (See Reproducible G-8R for game directions that students can take home.)

Teacher Reflection

My Experiences in Summarizing *101 and Out!*

We played *101 and Out!* today during class. After students had played the game a few times, I called them to the whole-group area to discuss a game scenario I had created. I showed them a partially played game:

Game 1

Round 1		20
Round 2	+	5
Total		25
Round 3	+	30
Total		55
Round 4	+	
Total		
Round 5	+	
Total		
Round 6	+	
Total		

The total so far was fifty-five and it was the third round. I let the students know that a 3 was rolled next. I asked them to think quietly for a moment about the decision they would make. I encouraged them to use the individual hundreds charts that were always available to students during whole-class discussions. After several moments, I asked them to turn to their discussion buddy and explain their thinking (in our classroom, discussion buddies are assigned ahead of time so no time is wasted while students try to find a partner). I asked students who were willing to share their thinking to raise their hand. I called on Omar.

Omar explained, "I would put the three in the tens place so the new total is eighty-five."

"Why do you think that is a good decision, Omar?" I asked.

"I have two rolls left, so maybe I could make smaller numbers next time," Omar responded.

"Thanks for sharing." I turned my attention to the class and asked, "Give me a thumbs-up if you agree with Omar. Omar said he would make the next two numbers small. Does anyone have another reason they would put the three in the tens place?" I paused to give students time to think. I then called on Jayce.

"I want to get close to one hundred and if I add three I would only be on fifty-eight, so I think adding thirty is better," Jayce explained.

"Jayce and Omar both decided to add thirty. Does anyone disagree with their idea and would rather add three?" I queried. We had been working on disagreeing respectfully with each other's ideas for several weeks. No one raised their hand to disagree. Malcolm spoke up, saying adding three would not help us get to one hundred very quickly. It appeared the whole class was in agreement, so I moved on to the next round. I told the class the next number rolled was a 1. The class seemed to wiggle in excitement. I reminded them to think quietly for a moment; I would let them know when to talk to their discussion buddy. After giving the students time to talk, I called on Grayson.

"I would add one to eighty-five because if I add ten, then I would be really, really close to one hundred and I still have a roll left," Grayson explained.

"OK, let me see if I understand. You would add one because you think adding ten is too much since you have one roll left," I restated. Grayson confirmed that this was his thinking, so I prompted him a little more by asking what his new total is. He told me eighty-six, so I put a counter on eighty-six on the hundreds chart. I asked Grayson to remind the class what the total would have been if he had added ten. When he said ninety-five, I put another counter on ninety-five. I wanted students to have a visual of both of the two outcomes.

"Grayson would rather add one since he has one more roll left. Will anyone else who would choose to add one explain their thinking?" I asked. I paused for a moment and then called on Felicity.

Felicity said, "I would add one, too, because I might roll a big number next time and go over one hundred."

"Does anyone disagree with adding one?" I asked.

"Yes, I disagree because when I add ten and get ninety-five, then the next turn I would put that number in the ones place." Jon said after I called on him.

"Felicity mentioned that the last roll might cause her to go over one hundred if she added ten in Round 5. Jon, what do you think about this?" I asked.

"Well, since I have ninety-five, I'm only five away from one hundred. I would cross my fingers and hope to not roll a six!" Jon exclaimed.

"I agree with Jon. It's probably not going to happen," Lucas added.

"What's probably not going to happen?" I asked Lucas to add on.

"We have lots of other numbers we could roll, like a one, two, three, four, or five. I hope we don't roll a six." Lucas expanded.

"So we have two different thoughts. Some of you would like to add a one because we don't know what the last roll will be. Some of you would like to add a ten and hope that the last roll is not a six. It sounds like all of you are really thinking about what makes sense. I have another question to ask you and it will help if our total is ninety-five, so I'm going to decide to add ten to our number. Our new total is ninety-five and we have one more roll. I want you to think quietly about this final question. What are you hoping to roll and why? Remember to think first, and then I'll let you know when to share with your discussion buddy." I gave everyone time to think and then had them turn and talk to their discussion buddies. After a few moments, I asked them to quiet down and show me with their fingers what number they hoped to roll. Almost the entire class flashed five fingers so I said, Almost all of us want to roll a five. I'm interested in hearing why. I want you to be a good listener because in a minute I'm going to ask you to write about your thinking."

Cody began by saying, "I want a five so I can add five. Ninety-five plus five is one hundred. I would be right on one hundred and win the game!"

"Who else would like to add on?" I asked.

"I wouldn't want a six because we would be over if we added six or sixty. And one, two, three, four would be OK, but five would be best." Jonah said.

"Why would five be best?" I asked. I knew that Jonah probably understood that by adding five to ninety-five he would have one hundred, but I wanted to give him an opportunity to verbalize his thinking, and give others an opportunity to listen to his thinking.

"Five is best because I would put it in the ones place. Ninety-five and five is one hundred, and I would be the winner!" Jonah exclaimed.

"OK, so adding five allows us to win the game, and we've heard a few people explain their thinking. I would like for you to go back to your seats and write about your thinking." I released the students back to their seats. They busily began writing about why they would want to roll a 5.

The Larger Difference

Overview

During this game, students find the difference between two numbers, using the hundreds chart to help with their calculations. Students have the opportunity to find the difference by adding or subtracting. Class discussions help connect the various methods students use to find the difference.

Related Lessons

You might teach the following lessons first:

▶ L-2 Building the Hundreds Chart (Version 2)

▶ L-6 Ten More or Ten Less

Key Questions

▶ What two numbers can we create?

▶ How would you determine the difference between the two numbers?

▶ Who has the larger difference? The smaller difference?

▶ What do you notice about all the differences you are finding?

Time

30 minutes

Materials

dice, 2 per pair of students

The Hundreds Chart, 1 per pair of students (Reproducible A)

counters, 2 per pair of students

pocket hundreds chart with removable numbers *or*

hundreds chart projected on screen or interactive whiteboard

The Larger Difference recording sheet, 1 per student (Reproducible 24)

optional: *The Larger Difference* Game Directions (Reproducible G-9R)

Teaching Directions

Introduce

1. Gather students together and display a pocket hundreds chart, a hundreds chart projected with a document camera or overhead, or a hundreds chart on an interactive whiteboard. Let students know they will be playing a game that will help them strengthen their skills to add and subtract efficiently on a hundreds chart.

2. Ask for a student volunteer to play with you. Tell students they will need two dice, a hundreds chart, and two small counters.

3. Roll the dice and tell students the numbers. Write the numbers down where everyone can see them. Explain that students will make two two-digit numbers and mark them on their hundreds chart with the counters. For example, if 3 and 5 are rolled, the possible numbers to create are thirty-five and fifty-three. If students roll the same number on each die, they may pick up the dice and roll again.

4. Explain that students will find the difference between the two numbers. Introduce the word *difference*, explaining that the difference is the space between two numbers, or how many numbers are in between two numbers. Give an example by drawing a number line and labeling it *1 2 3 4 5*. Write an *X* above the two and the five. Model counting the spaces between the numbers to find the difference.

5. Ask students to think for a moment about how they would determine the difference between the numbers.

> **Examples of Student Thinking**
>
> Teacher: Who has an idea about how to find the difference between your two numbers?

Student 1: You can start at the first number and count how many squares 'til you get the second number.

Teacher: How would you do that counting?

Student 1: Well, you could count by ones, but I would do it the fast way, by tens and then ones.

Teacher: Can you say more about that?

Student 1: I would just go down as many squares as I could (that's the adding tens part), then go over to get to the second number (that's the adding ones part).

Teacher: Who has another idea about finding the difference?

Student 2: You could do the same thing, only start at the second number and go up to the first.

6. Give them a few moments to talk with a partner before calling on a few students to explain how they found the difference between the two numbers (35 and 53). Record their thinking. Let students know that when they play the game, they will need to record their strategies (using the recording sheet), just like you are doing.

Examples of Student Thinking and Teacher Recording

Student 1 says, "I counted by ones."

Teacher records,

36	37	38	39	40	41	42	43	44	45	46	47	48	49	50	51	52	53
1	2	3	4	5	6	7	8	9	10	11	12	13	14	15	16	17	18

Student 2 says, "I counted by tens and then ones to the larger number."

Teacher records,

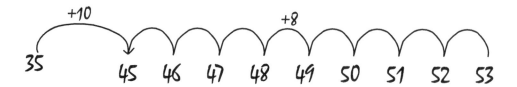

35   45 46 47 48 49 50 51 52 53

Student 3 says, "I counted back by tens and ones to the smaller number."

Teacher records,

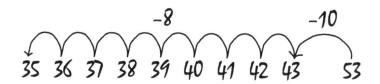

35 36 37 38 39 40 41 42 43   53

7. Next, introduce the following sentence frames:

    Sentence Frames

    My numbers were _____ and _____.

    The difference between my numbers is _____.

    The difference between my numbers was _____ [greater than, less than, or equal to] the difference between my partner's numbers.

8. Explain how to fill in the first two sentence frames by recording numbers used during the example:

    My numbers were 35 and 53.

    The difference between my numbers is 18.

    Let students know the last sentence frame will be completed after the second player takes his turn.

9. Pass the dice to the student volunteer, ask him to roll, create two two-digit numbers, and mark the numbers on the hundreds chart. Remind students that they need to find the difference between the two numbers. Ask them to think about how they would find the difference. Give the class a few moments to think before asking them to share their thinking with a partner, then ask a few students to share their thinking.

10. As students share their thinking, record their strategies where everyone can see them. Introduce the sentence frames for the volunteer, and complete the first two sentences. Next, point to the second sentence frames for each player and ask students to think about which difference was larger.

> Teacher: My difference was eighteen. Our volunteer's difference was forty-five. Think quietly for a moment about who has the larger difference. (Pause.) Turn and talk to your discussion buddy about who has the larger difference and how you knew. (Pause for a few moments.) Dustin, can you tell us who has the larger difference?

> Dustin: Forty-five is larger because eighteen has only one ten and forty-five has four tens.

> Teacher: So, we would read the volunteer's last sentence frame this way: *The difference between my numbers was greater than the difference between my partner's numbers.* Let's look at my sentence frame. Think quietly for a moment about how we would complete my sentence frame. (Pause.) Now turn and talk to your discussion buddy about how to complete my sentence frame. (Pause for a few moments.) Raul, how would you complete my sentence frame?

> Raul: You would say "less than."

Teaching Tip

Discussion Buddies

Oftentimes, students don't know who to turn to when teachers ask them to talk to a partner. To save time and alleviate any issues that might arise, assign "discussion buddies" before class discussions. Consider keeping the discussion buddies for several weeks so students become comfortable with their partner. Then switch buddies so students have opportunities to work with other classmates.

Teaching Tip

Class Games

If students seem confused about the game or would benefit from more discussions, play the game as a class a few more times. Use the key questions listed at the beginning of this game to promote class discussions.

Teacher: Can you say that using the sentence frame?

Raul: The difference between your numbers is less than the difference between your partner's numbers.

Use this information to complete the last sentence frame, using the phrases *greater than*, *less than*, or *equal to*.

11. Tell students they will play five total rounds. The person who has the larger difference more often is the winner.

Explore

12. Pass out dice, a hundreds chart, and two counters to each pair of students, and a recording sheet to each student (Reproducible 24). Remind students to record their strategies for finding the difference on the back of the recording sheet before completing the sentence frames.

13. As students play, observe the computation strategies they are using to find the difference. In one classroom there may be a variety of strategies, ranging from simplistic (like

Teaching Tip

Managing the Use of Dice
Using dice can be problematic if students are rolling them across the entire floor or throwing them across tables. To prevent such scenarios, give each group of students a 6-by-6-inch square of soft foam or cotton batting, and tell students they will lose their turn if they roll the dice off the foam. Setting such parameters decreases chaos (rolling—and in some cases, flying!—dice) and maintains control in the classroom.

Teaching Tip

If Players Finish Early
If partners finish a game (five rounds), ask them to play with another partner. Ask them to consider which numbers help them score a larger difference.

FIGURE G-9.1 Amiya rolls a 5 and a 3, and places her counters on thirty-five and fifty-three while Skylar looks on.

counting on by ones) to more advanced strategies (like using mental math). Encourage students to use a strategy that makes asense for them. Look for opportunities to help students develop more efficient strategies.

FIGURE G-9.2 Amiya writes her numbers on the sentence frame before finding the difference between thirty-five and fifty-three.

FIGURE G-9.3 Kendall and Steven work cooperatively to place their counters and find the difference.

A Child's Mind . . .

The Relationship Between Addition and Subtraction

When asking students if each strategy will result in the same difference, do not be surprised if many students believe it will result in two different answers. Young learners are still developing an understanding of how addition and subtraction relate.

Summarize

14. After students have completed at least one game (five rounds), ask students to put the dice away, leave their recording sheets at their tables or desks, and come to the whole-group area. Students may bring their individual hundreds charts if they desire.

15. Begin by telling students that you noticed several strategies for finding the difference: one was counting or adding up from the smaller number and one was counting or subtracting from the larger number. Ask students if they think each strategy will result in the same difference.

16. Roll the dice, create two two-digit numbers, mark them on the hundreds chart, and tell students you are interested in thinking more about adding up from the smaller number or subtracting from the larger number. Let's say the two numbers are twenty-four and forty-two.

17. Ask students to think about how they would find the difference between twenty-four and forty-two. Give them a few moments to think, and then have them talk to their partner. Ask for a show of hands of students who started from twenty-four, and call on one of those students.

18. As the student shares his thinking, record his strategy where everyone can see it. Record using an open number line and also a partial hundreds chart:

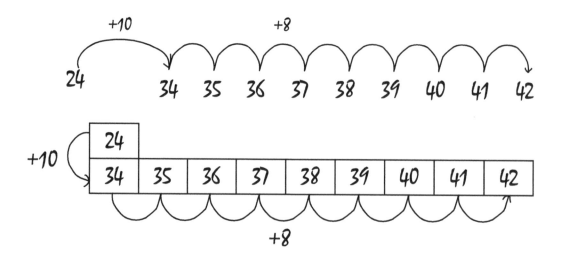

19. Connect to a number sentence by asking students, "What number did we start with?" Record *24*. Ask, "How much did we add?" Record *+ 18*. Ask, "What number did we end with?" and record *= 42*. The final recording will look like this:

$$24 + 18 = 42$$

20. Ask for a show of hands of students who started from the number forty-two. Call on one of those students. (If no one raises their hand, work as a class to subtract from forty-two to twenty-four.)

21. As the student shares her thinking, record it for everyone to see. Record using an open number line and also a partial hundreds chart:

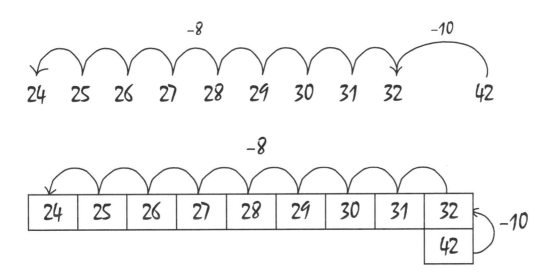

22. Connect to a number sentence. Ask, "What number did we start with?" Record *42*. Ask, "How much did we subtract?" Record *– 28*. Ask, "What number did we end up with?" Record *= 24*. The final recording will look like this:

$$42 - 18 = 24$$

Math Matters!

Differences

The only differences students will be able to come up with are nine, eighteen, twenty-seven, thirty-six, and forty-five. Some students will be intrigued with this finding. Encourage them to find all the pairs of numbers that yield a difference of nine, eighteen, twenty-seven, and so forth. Ask them what they notice about number pairs that yield a difference of nine compared with number pairs that yield a larger difference (all number pairs that yield a difference of nine are *consecutive numbers*).

Homework

For homework, send materials and game directions see Reproducible G-9R *The Larger Difference* home with a note attached asking parent and child to play the game one time (five rounds). Request that the recording sheet (Reproducible 24) and the student's strategies for finding the difference between the two numbers be returned to class.

23. Ask students, "What do you notice when you look at the strategies and number sentences?" Facilitate a class discussion, connecting the relationship between addition and subtraction.

Examples of Student Thinking

Student 1 observes, "The number sentences use the same numbers."

Teacher responds, "When we add up or subtract from the same numbers, the difference is the same. Each time the difference was eighteen."

Student 2 says, "The hundreds chart looks the same except opposite."

Teacher responds, "Yes, we are adding or subtracting the same amount. The only change is where we started on the hundreds chart."

Student 3 observes, "I'm better at adding up from a number."

Teacher responds, "Adding up or subtracting from are both efficient strategies. Use the one that makes the most sense to you. If you want to use a new strategy, try it out and ask for help if you need to."

24. If time allows, repeat the process for one more set of numbers, or begin the next class by spending a few minutes revisiting the ideas.

Teacher Reflection

My Experiences with Student Recordings for *The Larger Difference*

It's important that students know how to represent their thinking using numbers and words. They gain confidence doing this as you listen to them explain their thinking and then model how to record it. It's also important that students have opportunities to share their thinking and recording methods with other students. In this way, different methods of recording become public in the classroom and can be accessed by all students. The following photos depict strategies representing the range of thinking and recording in a typical classroom.

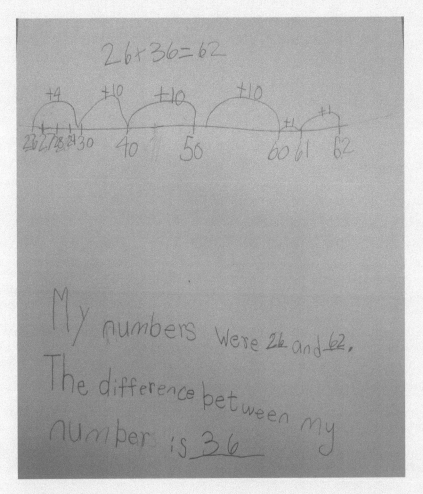

FIGURE G-9.4 Skylar's recording shows that she moves fluently between jumps of ones and tens to find the difference efficiently.

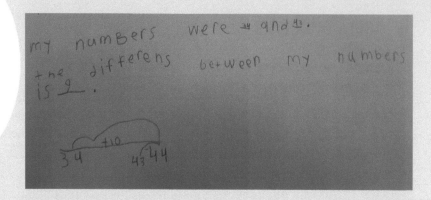

FIGURE G-9.5 In Kendall's recording, he makes a jump of ten, then jumps back one on the number line to get to forty-three, for a total difference of nine.

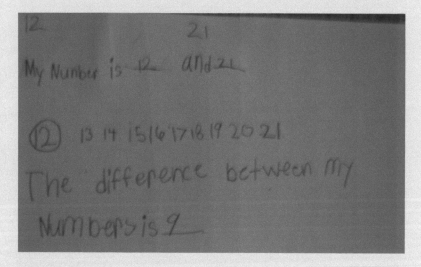

FIGURE G-9.6 In Amiya's recording, she counts by ones to find her difference of nine.

How Far Away?

Overview

During this game, students use the landmark number of one hundred to explore other numbers and their relationships to one hundred. Students get the opportunity to experience adding tens and ones to numbers. Students also gain valuable experience connecting subtraction and addition.

Related Lessons

You might teach the following lessons first:

▶ L-2 Building the Hundreds Chart (Version 2)

▶ L-3 Arrow Arithmetic

▶ L-6 Ten More or Ten Less

Key Questions

▶ How far from one hundred is the number? How do you know?

▶ What is similar about the strategies? What is different?

▶ Would you rather add up from the number or subtract from one hundred? Why?

Time

30 minutes

Materials

dice, 3 per pair of students

The Hundreds Chart (Reproducible A), 1 per pair of students

counters, 6 per pair of students (see How to Use This Resource, page xix)

pocket hundreds chart with removable numbers *or*

hundreds chart projected on screen or interactive whiteboard

optional: *How Far Away?* Game Directions (Reproducible G-10R)

Math Matters!

How Many Numbers Are Possible?

Mathematically it is possible to create six two-digit numbers when different numbers are rolled using three dice. It is likely that, as a class, students will find all six numbers during the introduction to the game. During the exploration phase, when students work with a partner, they may only find a few of the numbers. It is not mandatory that they find all the numbers because the purpose of the activity is for students to work on finding the difference.

Teaching Directions

Introduce

1. Introduce the game. Explain to students that they will roll three dice, create two-digit numbers, and figure out how far from one hundred a few of the numbers are.

2. Pass out copies of The Hundreds Chart (Reproducible A), one to each pair of students.

3. Model the game. Roll the three dice and record the numbers rolled where everyone can see them.

4. Ask students to work with a partner and create several two-digit numbers using the numbers rolled. For example, if you roll a 3, a 4, and a 1, students may create the numbers thirty-four, thirty-one, forty-two, forty-one, thirteen, or fourteen.

5. After a few moments, call on several students to share the numbers they created with their partner. Mark the numbers on the pocket hundreds chart, on a chart projected with a document camera or overhead, or on an interactive whiteboard.

6. Point to a number and say, "In this activity, we're going to try to figure out the difference between the number and one hundred. The word *difference* means how far apart the numbers are."

7. Ask students to think about how they would solve the problem. Encourage them to use the hundreds chart they've been given and to talk with their partner about solution strategies.

8. Call on students to share while you record their thinking. Explain to students that as they share their strategy, you will use an open number line to record their thinking, and that the line or "jumps" is similar to when their finger is moving on a hundreds chart.

Example of Student Thinking and Teacher Recording

Student 1 says, "I put my finger on forty-two and counted over to fifty, which was eight and added tens until I landed on one hundred. I added five tens. Fifty and eight is fifty-eight."

Teacher records,

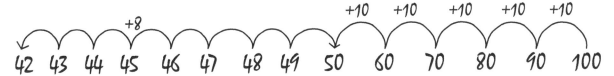

Student 2 notes, "I counted by tens from forty-two. So I went fifty-two, sixty-two, seventy-two, eighty-two, ninety-two, which was fifty, and then I counted over from ninety-two, which was fifty-eight."

Teacher records,

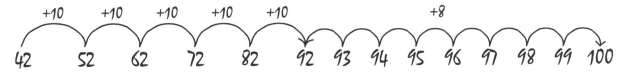

Differentiating Your Instruction

Gradual Release of Modeling
Some students may benefit from a gradual release model during which the teacher models a few strategies the first few times before asking the students to solve the next problem with a partner (and, finally, another problem on their own). When modeling strategies, think aloud so students hear the language used to describe the movement on the hundreds chart. Record your thinking so students see what they, in turn, are expected to record.

Math Matters!

The Open Number Line
The open number line is an efficient method for students to use to record their thinking. It supports flexible thinking because students can use it to add or subtract, and it allows them to begin with either the tens or the ones in either operation, depending on their thinking. The open number line also grows with the student as their thinking develops from simple counting strategies and moves to more complex counting strategies. An example of this would be a student who first counts by ones to find the difference between forty-two and fifty, but later knows the difference is eight and can make a jump of +8 instead of eight +1 jumps.

9. Ask students to review the two strategies and talk to their partner about what is similar and different about the two strategies. Use this opportunity to point out that either strategy yields the same difference. Ask students to confirm the difference and find where the difference (fifty-eight) is shown in the written strategy.

10. Typically, students would rather add on than subtract from a number. If subtracting from one hundred is not brought up by a student, consider modeling this strategy with the class. For example, "I wonder if we start on one hundred and subtract until we reach forty-two what the difference, or answer, would be? Do you think it will be the same? Let's try it! We'll start with our finger on one hundred and jump back until we get to forty-two. Count back by tens: one hundred, ninety, eighty, seventy, sixty, fifty. Stop here for a moment. If we count back another ten, we'll land on forty. Because we're trying to get to forty-two, forty would be too far back, so at this point we have to start counting back by ones—forty-nine, forty-eight, forty-seven, forty-six, forty-five, forty-four, forty-three, forty-two. Now let's count to see how many steps we took backward. We went back five tens, or fifty, and eight ones, making fifty-eight steps back." Some students may seem surprised that adding on from forty-two and subtracting from one hundred yield the same difference or answer. Consider recording this answer so students can see the similarities with the previous adding-up strategies:

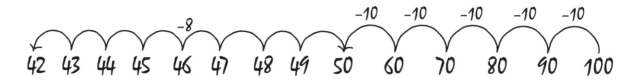

11. Pick another number that is marked on the hundreds chart and ask students to use their hundreds charts to find the difference. Encourage them to use one of the previously discussed strategies and talk with their partner about their thinking.

12. Call on students to share their thinking. Record their thinking. Repeat using an open number line.

13. Tell students that after finding the difference between one hundred and two rolls, students should pick the dice up and roll again. Roll the dice and record the numbers rolled.

14. Ask students to turn to their partner and create several two-digit numbers using the numbers rolled.

15. After a few moments, call on several students to share the numbers they created with their partner. Mark the new set of numbers on the displayed hundreds chart.

16. Pick a number and repeat the process of finding the difference. Choose another number and, again, repeat the process of finding the difference.

Differentiating Your Instruction

Finding the Difference Mentally

Depending on the level of learners in your classroom, there may be some students who can begin finding the difference mentally. Encourage them to do so and record their thinking using an open number line or another method that makes sense to them. During the exploration, look for students who may benefit from being encouraged to think mentally about the problem.

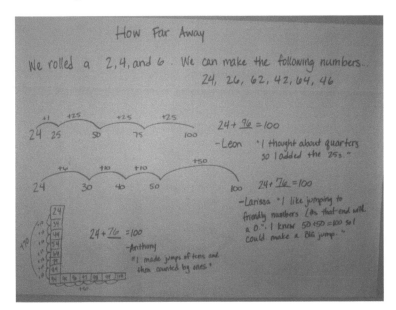

FIGURE G-10.1 An example of a teacher recording in a second-grade classroom. Second graders use a variety of strategies to find the difference. It is important for you to record their thinking so all students have access to their peers' thinking.

Explore

17. Explain to students they will now play the game with a partner. Review the directions and post them where all students can see them.

How Far Away? Game Directions

1. Roll three dice.

2. Create two-digit numbers and mark them on the hundreds chart.

3. Pick two of the numbers and find the difference between the numbers and one hundred.

4. Record your thinking.

5. Repeat the process.

18. Pass out hundreds charts, dice, and counters for students to use to mark their hundreds chart.

19. As students work on the activity, walk from group to group, asking the key questions listed at the beginning of this game. Encourage students to check their answer by also subtracting from one hundred.

Teaching Tip

From Partners to Solo

The purpose of having students work in partnerships during this game is to promote discussions about their thinking and about strategies for finding the difference. Students gain valuable information when they hear their peers thinking, and they solidify their own thinking when they verbalize their own thinking. Later, students can engage in this activity on their own. The purpose of working solo is to give students computation practice. The activity can then be taken up for a grade or assessment.

Teaching Tip

Managing the Use of Dice

Using dice can be problematic if students are rolling them across the entire floor or throwing them across tables. To prevent such scenarios, give each group of students a 6-by-6-inch square of soft foam or cotton batting, and tell students they will lose their turn if they roll the dice off the foam. Setting such parameters decreases chaos (rolling—and in some cases, flying!—dice) and maintains control in the classroom.

Summarize

20. Ask students to return the dice and hundreds charts before beginning a whole-class discussion. Gather students together.

21. Use the numbers marked on the hundreds chart from when you introduced the game. Choose a number (in this case, use thirty-one) and ask students to find the difference. Call on one student and record his thinking. If he uses addition, ask if anyone can use subtraction to solve the problem; scribe that student's thinking.

22. Point to the addition strategy and name it by saying, "This strategy is called adding on or finding the missing addend. We can write a number sentence or equation. What number did we start with?" Record *31*. "We added something to that number to reach one hundred." Record + __ = *100*. The final recording may look something like this:

$$31 + \underline{} = 100$$

23. Point to the blank and tell students, "In addition problems, the numbers we add are called *addends*. In this problem, one is missing, so we call it a *missing addend* problem."

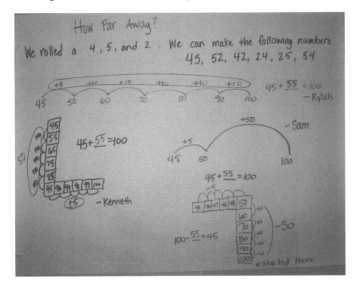

FIGURE G-10.2 Mrs. Conklin noticed that second graders in this class seemed more comfortable with finding the missing addend. She introduced using subtraction to find the difference, and they discussed how it was similar and different compared with one student's (Kenneth's) strategy.

Math Matters!

Connecting Addition and Subtraction

It is important for teachers to connect the relationship between addition and subtraction when working with multiple-digit numbers. *How Far Away?* offers an opportunity for students to experience how the difference stays the same whether they add on or subtract from. When you foster that thinking about adding on, students begin to calculate mentally with greater ease. Recording the equations and facilitating a class discussion helps students to begin to make these complex connections among operations. To read more about the connection between addition and subtraction, we recommend *Math Matters* by Suzanne Chapin and Art Johnson (Scholastic, 2006).

Homework

For homework, send materials and game directions (see Reproducible G-10R *How Far Away?*) home with a note attached asking parent and child to play the game three times, and to return the student's recording sheet to class.

24. Point to the subtraction problem and name it by saying, "This strategy is called *subtracting from* or *finding the missing number*. We can write a number sentence or equation. This time, what number did we start with?" Record *100*. "We subtracted something from one hundred to reach thirty-one." The final recording may look something like this:

$$100 - \underline{} = 31$$

25. Point to the blank and tell students, "We didn't know when we started what we were subtracting until we reached thirty-one."

26. Ask students to compare with their partner the equations and strategies they recorded. Encourage them to discuss what is similar and what is different.

27. Close by saying, "Addition and subtraction are related to each other. Some of you will feel more comfortable adding on from a number, whereas others of you will want to subtract from a number. I encourage you to try both and see which one feels most efficient or most comfortable to you."

Reproducibles

In addition to being available in this resource, downloadable printable versions are available online. See page xx for detailed access and registration instructions.

The following reproducibles are referenced and used with individual Lessons and Games:

Reproducible   1   Arrow Clue Cards: Sets A–C   183

Reproducible   2   Spinners: One Less or One More and –1 or +1   186

Reproducible   3   Blank Counting Board: 1–20   187

Reproducible   4   Blank Counting Board: 1–30   188

Reproducible   5   Blank Counting Board: 1–50   189

Reproducible   6   Numbered Counting Boards: 1–20   190

Reproducible   7   Numbered Counting Boards: 1–30   191

Reproducible   8   Numbered Counting Board: 1–50   192

Reproducible   9   Teacher Checklist: One More or One Less   193

Reproducible 10   Teacher Checklist: Ten More or Ten Less   194

Reproducible 11   Hundreds Chart Riddles: Sets A–C   195

Reproducible 12   Missing Number Puzzles: Sets 1–4   198

Reproducible 13   Missing Number Puzzles Assessment   202

Reproducible 14   From Here to There Word Problems   203

Reproducible 15   Number Chart Bingo! Cards   204

Reproducible 16   Fill It Up! Cards   210

Reproducible 17   Mystery Squares Masks: Sets A–D   211

Reproducible 18   Race to 100: Fives Strips   215

Reproducible 19   Race to 100: Tens Strips   216

Reproducible 20   Race to 100: Action Cards   217

Reproducible 21   Race to 100: Question Cards   218

Reproducible 22   101 and Out! Recording Sheet   219

Reproducible 23   101 and Out! Assessment Sheet   220

Reproducible 24   The Larger Difference Recording Sheet   221

The following reproducibles are referenced and used throughout the book:

Reproducible A   The Hundreds Chart (1–100)   222

Reproducible B   The Fifty Chart (1–50)   223

Reproducible C   101–200 Chart   224

Reproducible D   10-by-10 Grid   225

Reproducible E   10-by-5 Grid   226

The following Game Directions are referenced in individual games:

Reproducible G-1R   Number Chart Bingo! Game Directions   227

Reproducible G-2R   Too High, Too Low Game Directions   228

Reproducible G-3R   Fill It Up! Game Directions   229

Reproducible G-4R   Mystery Squares Game Directions   230

Reproducible G-5R   Don't Get Lost Game Directions   231

Reproducible G-6Ra   Hippety Hop, Cooperative Group Version Game Directions   232

Reproducible G-6Rb   Hippety Hop, Competitive Version Game Directions   233

Reproducible G-7R   Race to 100 Game Directions   234

Reproducible G-8R   101 and Out Game Directions   235

Reproducible G-9R   The Larger Difference Game Directions   236

Reproducible G-10R   How Far Away? Game Directions   237

Arrow Clue Cards: Sets A–C

48 ↓ → = ? Set A	**27** ↓ ↓ = ? Set A
60 ↑ ↑ = ? Set A	**32** ↓ ← = ? Set A
13 → ↓ = ? Set A	
97 ← ↑ = ? Set A	

Answer Key

(Answers are provided for left column cards first, then right column.)

Clue #1: 59
Clue #2: 40
Clue #3: 24
Clue #4: 86
Clue #5: 47
Clue #6: 41

54 ↓→↓ = **?**

Set B

8 →↓↓ = **?**

Set B

15 ←←↑ = **?**

Set B

41 →↓→ = **?**

Set B

78 ↓→↑ = **?**

Set B

Answer Key

(Answers are provided for left column cards first, then right column.)

Clue #1: 75

Clue #2: 3

Clue #3: 29

Clue #4: 53

Clue #5: 79

Clue #6: 43

62 ↑→↑ = **?**

Set B

(Arrow Clue Cards, *continued*)

From *It Makes Sense! Using the Hundreds Chart to Build Number Sense* by Melissa Conklin and Stephanie Sheffield. Portsmouth, NH: Heinemann. © 2012 by Heinemann. May be photocopied for classroom use.

16 ↓↓→↑ **= ?**

Set C

29 ↓→↖ **= ?**

Set C

49 ↑↗←← **= ?**

Set C

36 ↙↓→→ **= ?**

Set C

62 ↘→↓ **= ?**

Set C

85 ←↑↗ **= ?**

Set C

ℹ **Answer Key**

(Answers are provided for left column cards first, then right column.)

Clue #1: 27
Clue #2: 28
Clue #3: 75
Clue #4: 65
Clue #5: 29
Clue #6: 57

Spinners: One Less or One More and −1 or +1

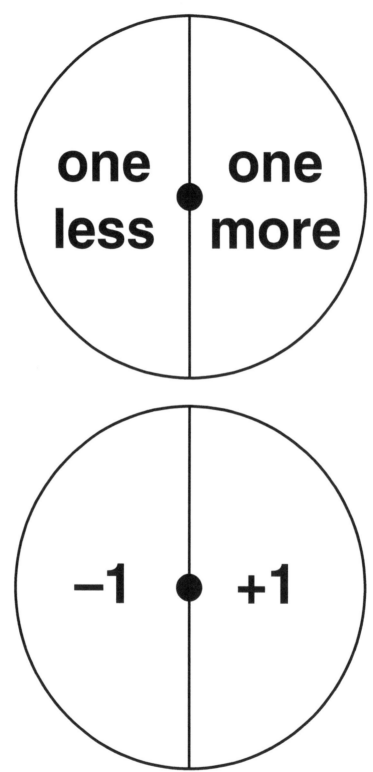

1. Pass out 1 large paper clip.

2. Use the tip of a pencil to keep the paper clip on the spinner.

3. Spin the paper clip while holding the pencil or have a partner hold the pencil while you spin the paper clip.

Blank Counting Board: 1–20

Blank Counting Board: 1–30

Blank Counting Board: 1–50

Numbered Counting Boards: 1–20

1	2	3	4	5	6	7	8	9	10
11	12	13	14	15	16	17	18	19	20

1	2	3	4	5	6	7	8	9	10
11	12	13	14	15	16	17	18	19	20

Numbered Counting Boards: 1–30

1	2	3	4	5	6	7	8	9	10
11	12	13	14	15	16	17	18	19	20
21	22	23	24	25	26	27	28	29	30

1	2	3	4	5	6	7	8	9	10
11	12	13	14	15	16	17	18	19	20
21	22	23	24	25	26	27	28	29	30

Numbered Counting Board: 1–50

1	2	3	4	5	6	7	8	9	10
11	12	13	14	15	16	17	18	19	20
21	22	23	24	25	26	27	28	29	30
31	32	33	34	35	36	37	38	39	40
41	42	43	44	45	46	47	48	49	50

From *It Makes Sense! Using the Hundreds Chart to Build Number Sense* by Melissa Conklin and Stephanie Sheffield. Portsmouth, NH: Heinemann. © 2012 by Heinemann. May be photocopied for classroom use.

Teacher Checklist: One More or One Less

Student Name and Date	Knew Answer Instantly	Used a Strategy Like Counting from a Benchmark Number	Used the Hundreds Chart	Used the Hundreds Chart and Counted from One	Was Not Able to Find the Correct Number

Teacher Checklist: Ten More or Ten Less

Student Name and Date	Knew Answer Fairly Quickly	Used the Hundreds Chart and Moved in Increments of Ten	Used the Hundreds Chart and Counted by One from the Number	Was Not Able to Find the Correct Number

Hundreds Chart Riddles: Sets A–C

Set A (Use with Reproducible A, The Hundreds Chart)

Riddle Set A, Number 1

1. My number is more than 5.
2. My number is smaller than 20.
3. My number has the digit 7 in it.
4. My number is 1 more than 6.

Riddle Set A, Number 2

1. My number is smaller than 23.
2. My number is more than 10.
3. My number has the digit 1 in it.
4. My number is 1 more than 13.

Riddle Set A, Number 3

1. My number is more than 9.
2. My number is smaller than 25.
3. My number has the digit 0 in it.
4. My number is the sum of 5 + 5.

Riddle Set A, Number 4

1. My number is smaller than 28.
2. My number is more than 10.
3. My number has the digit 2 in it.
4. My number is 20 + 5.

Set B (Use with Reproducible 8, Numbered Counting Board: 1–50)

Riddle Set B, Number 1

1. My number is more than 15.
2. My number is less than 40.
3. My number is even.
4. My number is the sum of 10 + 8.

Riddle Set B, Number 2

1. My number is less than 34.
2. My number is greater than 8.
3. My number is said when skip-counting by 5s.
4. My number is 10 + 10.

Riddle Set B, Number 3

1. My number is greater than 17.
2. My number is less than 43.
3. My number is odd.
4. My number is the sum of 10 + 10 + 3.

Riddle Set B, Number 4

1. My number is less than 16.
2. My number is greater than 4.
3. My number is said when skip-counting by 2s.
4. My number is the sum of 6 + 6.

Set C (Use with Reproducible A, The Hundreds Chart 1–100)

Riddle Set C, Number 1

1. My number is greater than 25.
2. My number is less than 88.
3. My number has a 4 in the 1s place.
4. My number is the sum of 24 + 20.

Riddle Set C, Number 2

1. My number is less than 72.
2. My number is greater than 36.
3. My number is said when skip-counting by 10s.
4. My number is the difference between 70 and 30.

Riddle Set C, Number 3

1. My number is greater than 48.
2. My number is less than 91.
3. My number is odd.
4. My number is the sum of 57 + 10.

Riddle Set C, Number 4

1. My number is less than 65.
2. My number is greater than 15.
3. My number has a 2 in the 10s place.
4. My number is the difference between 10 and 30.

Missing Number Puzzles: Sets 1–4

Set 1

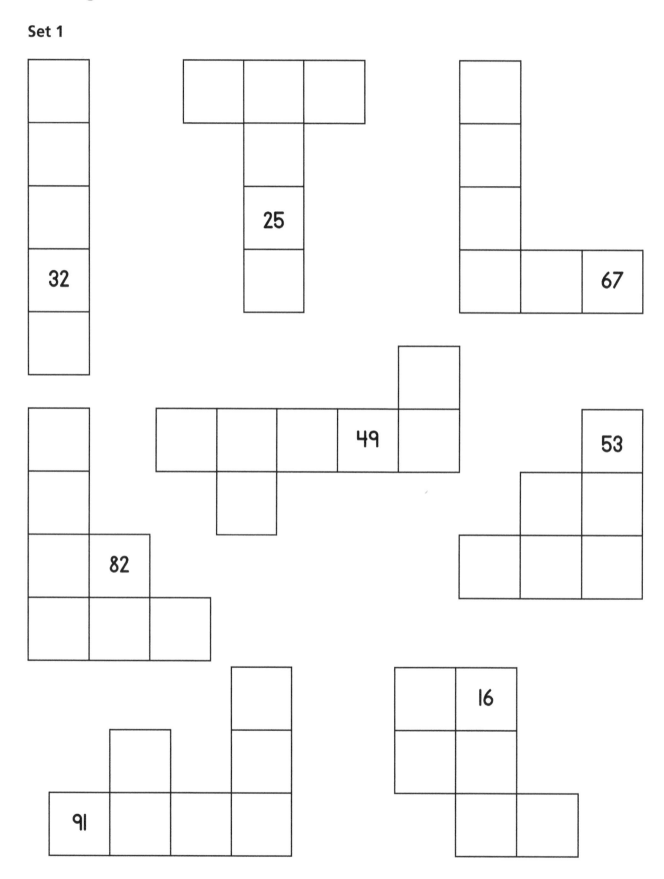

Set 2

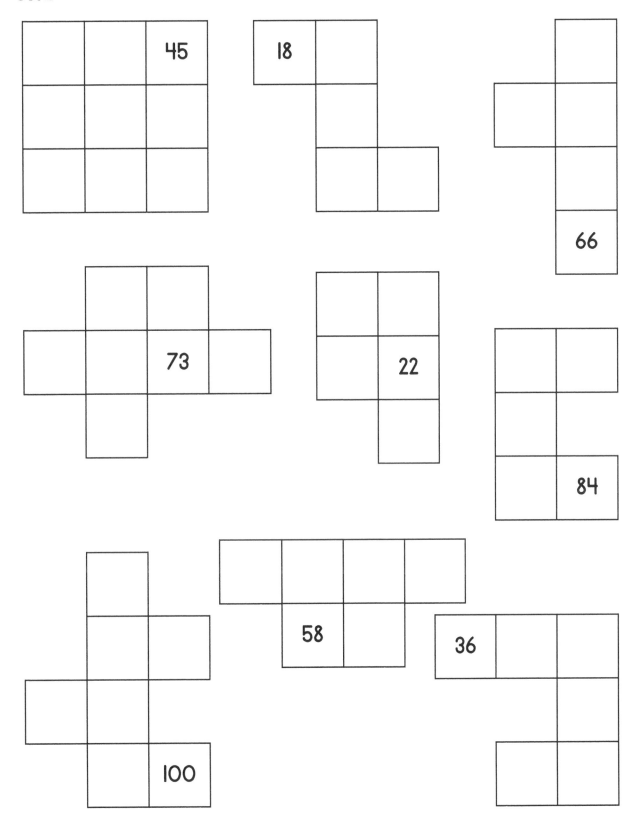

(Missing Number Puzzles, *continued*)

Set 3

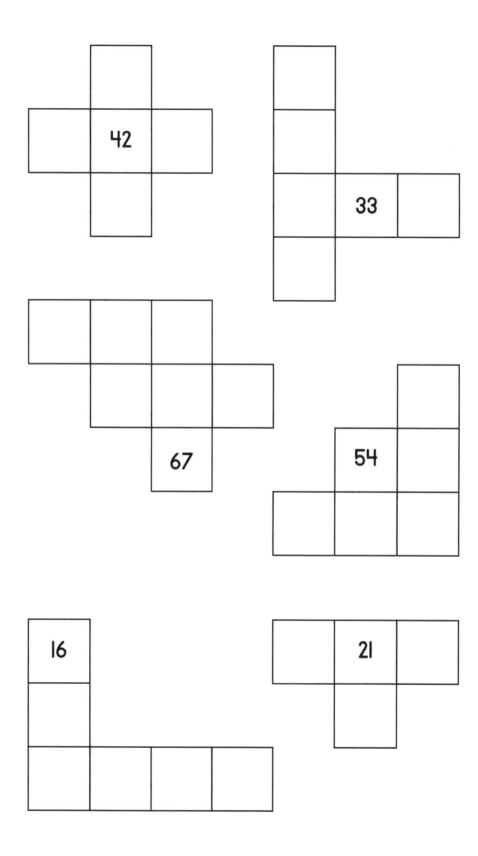

Set 4

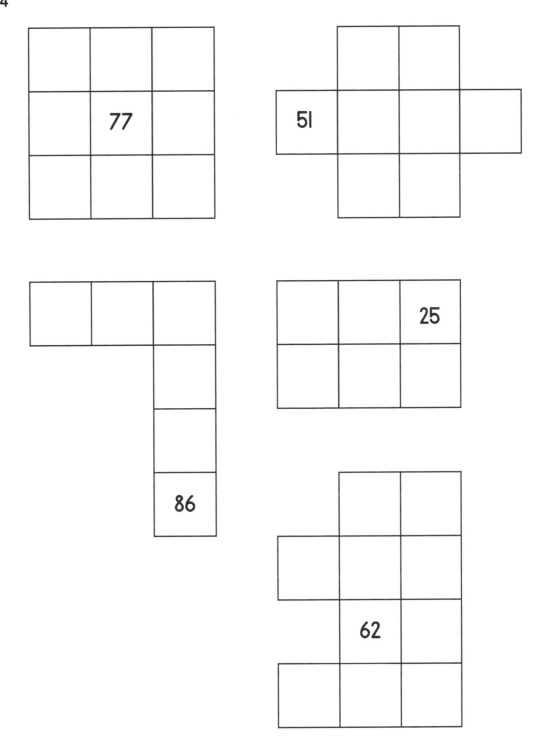

Missing Number Puzzles Assessment

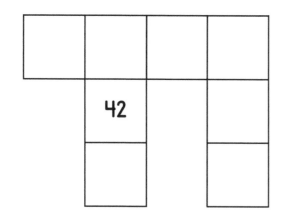

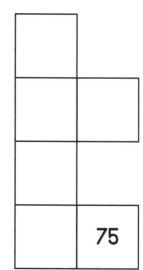

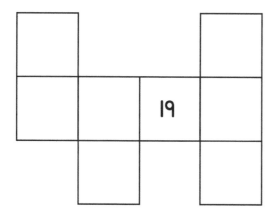

From Here to There Word Problems

Name: _____

1. The temperature in Fond du Lac, Wisconsin, is 48 degrees. The temperature in Houston, Texas, is 80 degrees. What is the difference in temperature between the two cities?

2. The temperature in Gary, Indiana, is 39 degrees. The temperature in North Little Rock, Arkansas, is 67 degrees. What is the difference in temperature between the two cities?

3. The temperature in Colorado Springs, Colorado, is 32 degrees. The temperature in Spring, Texas, is 85 degrees. What is the difference in temperature between the two cities?

4. The temperature in Washington, DC, is 55 degrees. The temperature in El Paso, Texas, is 92 degrees. What is the difference in temperature between the two cities?

Number Chart Bingo! Cards

Set A: Kindergarten Set

The number that is 1 more than 24. (25)	The number that is 1 less than 16. (15)	A number you say when you count by twos. (2 through 48, even numbers)
The number that is 10 and 1 more. (11)	The number that comes between 17 and 19. (18)	A number between 20 and 25. (21, 22, 23, 24)
A number that is less than 10. (1 through 9)	A number that is more than 20. (21 through 50)	The number that is 2 more than 8. (10)
5 + 5 (10)	The number that comes between 7 and 9. (8)	The number that is 1 more than 30. (31)
The number that is 1 less than 28. (27)	The number that is greater than 32 and less than 34. (33)	The number that is 1 more than 46. (47)

A number you say when you count by fives. (5, 10, 15, 20, 25, 30, 35, 40, 45, 50)	The number that is 26 and 1 more. (27)	The number that is 1 less than 50. (49)
A number that is more than 30. (31 through 50)	A number in the 40s. (40 through 49)	The number that is 1 more than 42. (43)
The number that comes between 12 and 14. (13)	The number that is 1 more than 19. (20)	A number in the 30s. (30 through 39)
The number that is 1 less than 42. (41)	The last number on the chart. (50)	A number that is 1 less than 2. (1)

(Number Chart Bingo! Cards, *continued*)

Set B: First Grade Set

The number that is 2 more than 6. (8)	A number you say when you count by tens. (10, 20, 30, 40, 50)	The number that is the sum of 5 and 2. (7)
The difference between 8 and 5. (3)	The sum of 5 + 5. (10)	The number that is 1 more than 12. (13)
A number you say when you count by fives. (5, 10, 15, 20, 25, 30, 35, 40, 45, 50)	The number that comes between 21 and 23. (22)	The number that is 10 more than 35. (45)
The difference between 10 and 8. (2)	The number that is 1 more than 39. (40)	A number you say when you count by twos. (all even numbers up to 50)
The number that is double 6. (12)	An odd number. (all odd numbers up to 49)	A number in the 30s. (30 through 39)

The number that is 1 more than 14. (15)	The number that is 2 less than 39. (37)	The number that is 10 more than 16. (26)
The number that is 6 and 3 more. (9)	The number that is 10 less than 50. (40)	The number that is 2 less than 3. (1)
The largest number on the board. (50)	The number that is 5 less than 50. (45)	The number that is 1 more than 17. (18)
A number that is more than 21 and less than 29. (22, 23, 24, 25, 26, 27, 28)		

Set C: Second Grade Set

A two-digit number that is less than 50 and greater than 48. (49)	An odd number in the 30s row. (31, 33, 35, 37, 39)	A number you say when you count by fives. (5, 10, 15, 20, 25, 30, 35, 40, 45, 50)
The number that ends in 0 and is between 20 and 40. (30)	The number that is 4 tens and 6 ones. (46)	The number you say when you count by twos 7 times. (14)
The number that is 10 more than 13. (23)	The number that is 20 less than 48. (28)	The number that is 1 more than 24. (25)
The number that is 5 less than 10. (5)	The number that is 3 tens and 6 ones. (36)	The number that is 10 more than 22. (32)
A number that is between 15 and 19. (16, 17, 18)	An even number in the 40s. (42, 44, 46, 48)	The number that is more than 6 and less than 8. (7)

The number that is 2 less than 8. (6)	A number less than 10. (1, 2, 3, 4, 5, 6, 7, 8, 9)	The number that is the same as 2 tens and 9 ones. (29)
The number that is double 11. (22)	The number that is 10 less than 25. (15)	An even number that is more than 12 and less than 20. (14, 16, 18)
The number that is 10 more than 34. (44)	The number that is 20 less than 41.	

Fill It Up! Cards

+1	+1	+1	−1	−1
−1	+2	+2	+2	−2
−2	−2	+10	+10	+10
−10	−10	−10	+20	+20
+20	−20	−20	−20	+1

Mystery Squares Masks: Sets A–D

Mask A

This reproducible features nine copies of Mask A; cut around the perimeter of each to form nine copies.

?	?
?	?

Mask B

This reproducible features nine copies of Mask B; cut around the perimeter of each to form nine copies.

?	?	?
?	■	?
?	?	?

?	?	?
?	■	?
?	?	?

?	?	?
?	■	?
?	?	?

?	?	?
?	■	?
?	?	?

?	?	?
?	■	?
?	?	?

?	?	?
?	■	?
?	?	?

?	?	?
?	■	?
?	?	?

?	?	?
?	■	?
?	?	?

?	?	?
?	■	?
?	?	?

Mask C

This reproducible features nine copies of Mask C; cut around the perimeter of each to form nine copies.

Mask D

This reproducible features six copies of Mask D; cut around the perimeter of each to form six copies.

?	?	?
?	?	?
?	?	?
?	?	?
?	?	?

?	?	?
?	?	?
?	?	?
?	?	?
?	?	?

?	?	?
?	?	?
?	?	?
?	?	?
?	?	?

?	?	?
?	?	?
?	?	?
?	?	?
?	?	?

?	?	?
?	?	?
?	?	?
?	?	?
?	?	?

?	?	?
?	?	?
?	?	?
?	?	?
?	?	?

Race to 100: Fives Strips

5	5
5	5
5	5
5	5
5	5

Race to 100: Tens Strips

10

10

10

10

10

10

10

Race to 100: Action Cards

+10	+10	+10
+10	+10	+20
+20	+20	+30
+30	+5	+5
−10	−10	−10
−20	−5	−5

Race to 100: Question Cards

How many more do you need to reach 100?	How many more do you need to reach 100?	How many more do you need to reach 100?
How far from 50 are you?	How far from 50 are you?	How far from 50 are you?
What is 10 *more* than what you have right now?	What is 10 *more* than what you have right now?	What is 10 *more* than what you have right now?
What is 10 *less* than what you have right now?	What is 10 *less* than what you have right now?	What is 10 *less* than what you have right now?
What is 5 *more* than what you have right now?	What is 5 *more* than what you have right now?	What is 5 *more* than what you have right now?
What is 5 *less* than what you have right now?	What is 5 *less* than what you have right now?	What is 5 *less* than what you have right now?

101 and Out! Recording Sheet

Name: _____

Game 1

Round 1 _____

Round 2 + _____

Total _____

Round 3 + _____

Total _____

Round 4 + _____

Total _____

Round 5 + _____

Total _____

Round 6 + _____

Total _____

Game 2

Round 1 _____

Round 2 + _____

Total _____

Round 3 + _____

Total _____

Round 4 + _____

Total _____

Round 5 + _____

Total _____

Round 6 + _____

Total _____

Game 3

Round 1 _____

Round 2 + _____

Total _____

Round 3 + _____

Total _____

Round 4 + _____

Total _____

Round 5 + _____

Total _____

Round 6 + _____

Total _____

101 and Out! Assessment Sheet

Ray and Mei Li were playing a game of *101 and Out!* This is their recording sheet so far:

Game 1

Round 1	30
Round 2 +	6
Total	36
Round 3 +	20
Total	56
Round 4 +	5
Total	61
Round 5 +	
Total	
Round 6 +	
Total	

In Round 5, they rolled a 3, and in Round 6 they rolled a 2. How do you think they should play these rolls and why?

Round 5:   30 or 3   Circle one

Why?

Round 6:   20 or 2   Circle one

Why?

The Larger Difference Recording Sheet

From *It Makes Sense! Using the Hundreds Chart to Build Number Sense* by Melissa Conklin and Stephanie Sheffield. Portsmouth, NH: Heinemann. © 2012 by Heinemann. May be photocopied for classroom use.

Name: _____

Round 1

My numbers are _____ and _____.

The difference between my numbers is _____.

The difference between my numbers was _____ the difference between my partner's numbers.

Round 2

My numbers are _____ and _____.

The difference between my numbers is _____.

The difference between my numbers was _____ the difference between my partner's numbers.

Round 3

My numbers are _____ and _____.

The difference between my numbers is _____.

The difference between my numbers was _____ the difference between my partner's numbers.

Round 4

My numbers are _____ and _____.

The difference between my numbers is _____.

The difference between my numbers was _____ the difference between my partner's numbers.

Round 5

My numbers are _____ and _____.

The difference between my numbers is _____.

The difference between my numbers was _____ the difference between my partner's numbers.

The Hundreds Chart (1–100)

1	2	3	4	5	6	7	8	9	10
11	12	13	14	15	16	17	18	19	20
21	22	23	24	25	26	27	28	29	30
31	32	33	34	35	36	37	38	39	40
41	42	43	44	45	46	47	48	49	50
51	52	53	54	55	56	57	58	59	60
61	62	63	64	65	66	67	68	69	70
71	72	73	74	75	76	77	78	79	80
81	82	83	84	85	86	87	88	89	90
91	92	93	94	95	96	97	98	99	100

The Fifty Chart (1–50)

1	2	3	4	5	6	7	8	9	10
11	12	13	14	15	16	17	18	19	20
21	22	23	24	25	26	27	28	29	30
31	32	33	34	35	36	37	38	39	40
41	42	43	44	45	46	47	48	49	50

101–200 Chart

101	102	103	104	105	106	107	108	109	110
111	112	113	114	115	116	117	118	119	120
121	122	123	124	125	126	127	128	129	130
131	132	133	134	135	136	137	138	139	140
141	142	143	144	145	146	147	148	149	150
151	152	153	154	155	156	157	158	159	160
161	162	163	164	165	166	167	168	169	170
171	172	173	174	175	176	177	178	179	180
181	182	183	184	185	186	187	188	189	190
191	192	193	194	195	196	197	198	199	200

10-by-10 Grid

10-by-5 Grid

Number Chart Bingo!

Objective

One person, the caller, calls out clues from the *Number Chart Bingo!* cards while other players cover a number on their board (1–50 chart) that fits the clue. The first player with a vertical, horizontal, or diagonal line of covered numbers across the number chart is the winner.

Materials

The FIfty Chart (1–50) (Reproducible B), 1 per student

counters, approximately 15 per student

1 set of *Number Chart Bingo!* cards (Reproducible 15)

Players

3 or more

Directions

1. Each player needs a game board (1–50 chart) and counters.

2. One person, the caller, calls out clues from the *Number Chart Bingo!* cards.

3. Players cover one number for each clue, if the clue fits one of the numbers showing on their board.

4. The game is over when one player has a Bingo, which is a straight line of marked numbers, either horizontally, vertically, or diagonally across the board.

Game Directions

Too High, Too Low

Objective

Students try to guess a number that one student (the hider) has chosen and written down. After each guess the players make, the hider gives a clue about whether the guess was too high or too low. She then marks the hundreds chart with a red and green counter to indicate the parameters of the possible solution. The game is over when the correct number is guessed.

Materials

The Hundreds Chart (1–100) (Reproducible A), 1 per player

red and green markers, such as transparent disks or tiles, or lima beans colored red and green, 1 of each color

Players

2 or more

Directions

1. The hider chooses a number, writes it down, and keeps it hidden.

2. The guessers take turns guessing numbers.

3. After each turn, the hider uses the phrase, "Your guess is too high" or "Your guess is too low."

4. The hider uses red markers to show guesses that are too high and green markers to show guesses that are too low.

5. When the number is guessed, the hider congratulates the group and shows the paper on which the number is written.

Homework

For homework, you can send materials and game directions home with a note attached asking the parent and child to play the game three times.

Fill It Up!

Overview

During this game, pairs of students take turns drawing a *Fill It Up!* card. The direction on the card tells the students how much to add to or subtract from one of the numbers already on their chart. In this way, they work together to fill their chart completely.

Materials

1 blank 10-by-10 Grid (Reproducible D)

2 sets of *Fill It Up!* cards (Reproducible 16)

2 number cubes

Players

2 players

Directions

1. Roll two number cubes and use them to make a two-digit number. Write that number where it belongs on the blank 10-by-10 grid. Check a completed hundreds chart to be sure the number you wrote is placed correctly.

2. Mix up the *Fill It Up!* cards and place them face down in a pile.

3. Take turns drawing one card from the pile and following the direction on the card to add or subtract from the numbers on the grid, then fill in the new number.

4. If you draw a card and cannot write a new number because it is already on the grid, draw a new card. If, after four draws, you cannot place a new number, the game is over.

Kindergarten Version

Use a 10-by-5 grid (Reproducible E) and remove the +10, −10, +20, and −20 cards from the *Fill It Up!* card set. Write the number 35 on the grid as a starting point for students.

Homework

For homework, can send materials and game directions home with a note attached asking the parent and child to play the game three times.

Game Directions

Mystery Squares

Objective

Partners take turns hiding a part of the hundreds chart with a mask. The other player figures out which numbers are covered and writes them on a student whiteboard or in his or her math journal. Both students check to determine whether the written numbers match the ones that were covered.

Materials

The Hundreds Chart (Reproducible A), 1 per student

Mystery Squares masks (Reproducible 17)

1 student whiteboard

1 dry-erase marker and 1 eraser *or*

1 math journal and 1 pencil

Players

2 players

Directions

1. One player is the hider and one is the guesser.

2. The guesser covers his eyes while the hider covers part of the chart with the mask.

3. The guesser records on the whiteboard (or in her student journal) the numbers that are covered by the mask.

4. The hider then removes the mask and both students check to determine whether the numbers the guesser recorded match the numbers the hider covered.

Homework

For homework, you can send materials and game directions home with a note attached asking the parent and child to play the game three times.

Don't Get Lost

Objective

Players take turns giving each other directions and guiding their movements on a hundreds chart. Together, they check each other's work.

Materials

The Hundreds Chart (Reproducible A), 1 per pair of students

a blank 10-by-10 Grid (Reproducible D), 1 per pair of students

1 counter per pair of students

Players

2 players

Directions

1. Player 1 gives directions while moving his finger on a filled-in hundreds chart.

2. Player 2 follows the directions by moving her counter on a blank 10-by-10 grid.

3. After giving three directions, Player 1 asks, "Where are you?" Player 2 responds by telling Player 1 on which space her counter is located.

4. Player 1 acknowledges that Player 2 is correct. If Player 2 is not correct, together the players retrace the directions on the blank chart to find the correct space.

5. Repeat Steps 1 through 4, with Players 1 and 2 changing roles during the game.

Homework

For homework you can send materials and game directions home with a note attached asking the parent and child to play the game three times.

Hippety Hop
Cooperative Group Version

Objective

Players work together to make the fewest hops to the target number. Players may take hops of one, ten, or one hundred. Players record the equations and the number of hops it took to reach the target number.

Materials

The Hundreds Chart (Reproducible A), 1 per pair of students

a sheet of paper, 1 per pair of students

Players

1 to 2 players

Directions

1. Using target numbers that have been assigned, make hops of one, ten, or one hundred to the target number.

2. Record the equation that matches the hops you made.

3. Count the hops and record it next to the equation.

4. Check to determine whether there is a way to reach the target number using fewer hops.

5. Repeat Steps 1 through 4 using a new target number.

Homework

For homework you can send materials and game directions home with a note attached asking parent and child to play the game three times.

Game Directions

Hippety Hop
Competitive Version

Objective

Players try to make the fewest hops to the target number they've pulled from a bag containing the numbers one through one hundred. Players may take hops of one, ten, or one hundred. Players record the equations and the number of hops it took to reach the target number. The player with the fewest hops wins the round.

Materials

The Hundreds Chart (Reproducible A)

a hundreds chart with the numbers cut apart into "target number" cards and placed into a bag, 1 per group of students

sheets of paper, 1 per group of students

Players

2 to 3 players

Directions

1. Using the number cards they have drawn, the players make hops of one, ten, or one hundred to the target numbers.

2. Players record the equation and number of hops made to reach the target number.

3. Players compare the number of hops each person took and determine who took the fewest hops.

4. The player with the fewest hops wins the round.

5. Play five rounds.

Homework

For homework you can send materials and game directions home with a note attached asking parent and child to play the game three times.

Game Directions

Race to 100

Objective

Players draw an action card and perform the action by placing the appropriate strips on a hundreds chart. They then draw a question card and answer the question. Play continues until a player gets to or goes over one hundred.

Materials

The Hundreds Chart (Reproducible A),
1 per player

fives and tens strips (Reproducibles 18 and 19)

Race to 100 Action Cards (Reproducible 20)

Race to 100 Question Cards (Reproducible 21)

Players

2 to 3 players

Directions

1. Players shuffle the action cards and place them in one pile. Players shuffle the question cards and place them in another pile. Players place the fives and tens strips so they can be reached easily, and then they set a hundreds chart in front of them.

2. Player 1 draws an action card and places the appropriate strips on his hundred chart. Then Player 1 draws a question card and answers the question.

3. Player 2 and/or Player 3 repeat Step 2, placing the appropriate strips on their hundreds chart and answering the question card.

4. Play continues until a player gets to or goes over one hundred.

Game Directions

101 and Out

Objective

Players roll a die and decide whether the number should be placed in the ones or tens place. After six rolls, the player that is closer to one hundred without going over is the winner.

Materials

dice

The Hundreds Chart (Reproducible A)

game counters

101 and Out! Recording Sheet (Reproducible 22)

optional: 101–200 Chart (Reproducible C)

Players

2 players

Directions

1. Player 1 rolls the die, decides whether he will put the number in the tens place or the ones place, and moves his counter to the number he created. After he writes the number on the recording sheet, he passes the die to Player 2.

2. Player 2 rolls the die, decides whether she will put the number in the tens place or the ones place, and moves her counter to the number she created. After she writes the number on the recording sheet, she passes the die back to Player 1.

3. Player 1 repeats the steps, this time adding the newly created number to the number from Round 1. Player 2 also repeats this process.

4. Play continues until both players have rolled the die six times.

5. Players 1 and 2 compare their total to see who is closer to one hundred without going over. This person is the winner.

Homework

For homework you can send materials and game directions home with a note attached asking parent and child to play the game three times and to return the *101 and Out!* recording sheet to class.

Game Directions

The Larger Difference

Objective

Players roll two dice and create two two-digit numbers. Players find the difference between the numbers and compare to determine who found the larger difference.

Materials

2 dice

The Hundreds Chart (Reproducible A)

2 small counters

The Larger Difference Recording Sheet (Reproducible 24), 1 copy for each player

Directions

1. Player 1 rolls the dice, creates two two-digit numbers, and uses the counters to mark the numbers on the hundreds chart. (If the same two numbers are rolled, the player needs to roll again.)

2. Player 1 finds the difference between the two numbers and records her strategy on the back of the recording sheet. Player 1 passes the dice to Player 2.

3. Player 2 rolls the dice, creates two two-digit number, and uses the counters to mark the numbers on the hundreds chart. (If the same two numbers are rolled, the player needs to roll again.)

4. Player 2 finds the difference between the two numbers and records his strategy on the back of the recording sheet.

5. Both players complete their own recording sheets. Play one game (five rounds). The winner is the person who has the largest difference most often.

Homework

For homework send materials and game directions home with a note attached asking parent and child to play the game one time (five rounds). Request that the recording sheet and the student's strategies for finding the difference between the two numbers be returned to school.

Game Directions

How Far Away?

Objective

Players roll three dice to create several two-digit numbers. These numbers are marked on the hundreds chart. Players pick two numbers to find the difference between those numbers and one hundred, and record their strategies.

Materials

3 dice

The Hundreds Chart (Reproducible A)

transparent counters or a dry-erase marker (depending on whether laminated chart is used)

sheet of paper

optional: laminated hundreds chart

Players

1 or more

Directions

1. Roll three dice.

2. Create several two-digit numbers and write them down. Mark them on a hundreds chart using transparent counters, or color the numbers on a laminated hundreds chart with a dry-erase marker.

3. Pick two of the numbers and find the difference between the numbers and one hundred.

4. Record your strategy using equations, open number lines, or partial drawings of the hundreds chart.

Homework

For homework send materials and game directions home with a note attached asking parent and child to play the game three times. Request the parent to return the student's recording sheet to school.

Index

A

addends, 179
addition
  101 and Out! game, 150–160
  communitative property of,
    148
  connecting with subtraction,
    87, 180
  example of student thinking,
    84
  Fill It Up! game, 111–116
  finding differences (*See Solving
    Comparison Problems*
    lesson)
  How Far Away? game, 173–180
  The Larger Difference
    game, 161–172
  Race to 100 game, 142–149
  relationship to subtraction, 167
  *Solving Comparison
    Problems* lesson, 80–88
  of two-digit numbers, 51
arranging, Bingo Card stack, 99
Arrow Arithmetic lesson, 20–27, 78
Arrow Clue Cars
  (Reproducible 1), 27
arrow clue practice with partner, 22
assessment
  formative, riddles as, 65
  Missing Number Puzzles
    Assessment, 76
  teacher checklists for,
    45–46, 56–57
assigning partners, 92

B

Blank Counting Board, 1–20
  (Reproducible 3), 37
Blank Counting Board, 1–30
  (Reproducible 4), 37
Blank Counting Board, 1–50
  (Reproducible 5), 37
brainstorming, 95
*Building a Wacky Hundreds
  Chart* lesson, 28–36
Building the Hundreds Chart lesson
  version 1, 6–11
  version 2, 12–19

C

calling on students, 87
Chapin, Suzanne H.
  *Math Matters: Understanding
    the Math You Teach,
    Grades K–8,* 67, 180
  *Using Math Talk to Help
    Students Learn,* 135
class discussions, 149, 176
class games, 165
classroom management,
  during math games,
  92–94
clue cards
  matching, 100
  open, discussing multiple
    numbers for, 100
clues, using, 120
coloring squares, 68
columns, for counting, 67
communitative property, 148
comparison
  of numbers, 91
  problem solving
    (*see Solving Comparison
    Problems* lesson)
competition, 16, 115, 138
computational fluency
  development, *Hippety
  Hop* game, 133–141
connections, making, 134
consecutive numbers, 170
consistency, importance
  of, 104
cooperative class games, 31
counters, 92, 103, v
counting
  by ones, 126
  space between numbers
    and, 82

D

decision-making, in lesson
  preparation, 7
decomposing numbers, *Race
  to 100* game, 142–149
desks, playing games at, 93
diagonal arrows, 27

dice, use of
  managing, 153, 165, 178
  three, 174
differences, finding, 170.
  *See also Solving Comparison
    Problems* lesson
  The Larger Difference
    game, 161–172
  mentally, 177
differentiation of instruction,
  135, 154
discussion buddies, 135,
  139–141, 146, 152
discussions, whole-class
  on *101 and Out!* game,
    157–160
  of game strategies, 151
  on lessons, 4–5
  on place-value concept,
    129–120
  recording students
    thinking and, 149
  in solidifying students
    understanding of peers
    thinking, 176
  on *Too High, Too Low,*
    109–110
disequilibrium, 176
document camera, 100
  Don't Get Lost game, 123–132
  Don't Get Lost Game Directions
    (Reproducible G-5R), 123,
    128

E

English language learners, 99
even/odd concept, *Number Chart
  Bingo!* game, 97–101
exploration phase of lesson, 3, 4.
  See also under specific lessons

F

Fill It Up! cards (Reproducible 16),
  111
Fill It Up! game, 95, 111–116
Fill It Up! Game Directions
  (Reproducible G-3R), 111, 115
finishing early, 88, 137, 166

first graders
   building the hundreds
      chart with, 10–11
   forward counting *vs.* backward
      counting sequences, 39
   lesson modifications for, 32
   Number Chart Bingo! game, 97–101
   symbols and, 105
floor, playing games at, 93
From Here to There Word Problems
   (Reproducible 14), 80, 88

G

games. *See* math games
geometric patterns, on
      hundreds chart, 55
greater than concept
   symbol for, 61
   Too High, Too Low game, 103–110

H

help seeking, 16
highlighting, 48
Hippety Hop game, 133–141
Hippety Hop Game Directions-
   competitive group version
   (Reproducible G-6Rb), 133, 138
Hippety Hop Game Directions-
   cooperative group version
   (Reproducible G-6Ra), 133, 138
homework, 108, 115, 122, 128,
   138, 148, 156, 170
How Far Away? game, 173–180
How Far Away? Game Directions
   (Reproducible G-10R), 173
hundreds chart, iv
   blank, 125
   building, 3, 6–19
   "cut outs," missing numbers as, 77
   description of, i
   filling in, 114
   filling in missing numbers in,
      91 (*see also Fill It Up!* game)
   individual, availability of, 146
   marking, 81, 83
   numbers, using a portion of, 29
   partially filled, use of, 81
   patterns on, 55
   pocket, i–ii

preparation of, 91–92
reason for using, ii–iii
Reducible A, 12, 13, 20
size of, i
touching, 23, 24
The Hundreds Chart
   (Reproducible A), 20, 37,
      47, 58, 59, 80, 88, 103, 117,
      123, 133, 142, 150, 161, 173
Hundreds Chart Riddles : Sets A–C
   (Reproducible 11), 58, 59
Hundreds Chart Riddles
   lesson, 58–65

I

identifying two-digit numbers, 91
incorrect answers, dealing with, 40
instruction, differentiation of.
   See under specific lessons
interactive whiteboard, use of,
   7, 8, 13, 15, 38, 39, 67, 70,
   98, 104, 151, 154, 155
introduction, for lesson, 3, 4. *See
   also under specific lessons*
Islas, Dana, *How to Assess While
   you Teach Math: Formative
   Assessment Practices and
   Lessons,* 45, 56

K

key questions, 4. *See also
   specific lessons*
kindergartners
   building the hundreds
      chart with, 10
   game modifications for, 116
   lesson modifications
      for, 17–19, 32
   Number Chart Bingo!
      game, 97–101
   number selection for, 39

L

The Larger Difference game,
   161–172
The Larger Difference Game
   Directions (Reproducible
   G-9R), 161

The Larger Difference Recording
   Sheet (Reproducible 24), 161
learning extensions. *See
   under specific lessons*
lesser than concept, *Too High,
   Too Low* game, 103–110
lessons. *See also specific lessons*
   design of, iii
   discussion on, 4–5
   key questions, v
   materials, iv–v (*See also
      under specific lessons*)
   overview (*See also under
      specific lessons*)
   overview of, iv
   purpose of, iv
   rationale for, 3
   "Related Lessons" section of, iv
   teacher's role in, 4–5
   time requirements for, 4
   "Time" section, iv
   use of, iv–v
Look, Quick! lesson, 66–72
losing, 95

M

magnitude of numbers, 153, 154
markers, transparent, iv
masks, for *Mystery Squares*
      game, 117
matching number cards, 42
materials. *See also under
      specific lessons*
   preparation, for math
      games, 91–92
   preparing for small groups, 41
math games
   classroom management
      during, 92–94
   materials preparation for, 91–92
   modeling, importance of, 94–95
   pieces for, 93–95
   purpose of, 91, iv
   when to use, 91
   winning/losing, 95
   without winners, 95
math stations, 27
mental image of hundreds charts
   Don't Get Lost game, 123–132
   Mystery Squares game, 117–122

missing addend problem, 179
Missing Number Puzzles
    (Reproducible 12), 73, 75
Missing Number Puzzles
    Assessment (Reproducible 13),
    73, 76
Missing Number Puzzles
    lesson, 73–79
modeling, 153
    balancing discussion
        time during, 152
    gradual release of, 175
    math games, importance of, 94–95
modifications, for lessons/games.
        See under specific lessons/games
modifying lessons, 61
Mystery Squares game, 117–122
Mystery Squares Game Directions
    (Reproducible G-4R), 117, 122
Mystery Squares Masks A and B
    (Reproducible 17), 117, 120

N

National Council of Teachers
    of Mathematics (NCTM),
    *Principles and Standards for
    School Mathematics,* iii
Number Chart Bingo! cards
    (Reproducible 15), 97
Number Chart Bingo! game, 97–101
Number Chart Bingo! Game
    Directions (Reproducible
    G-1R), 97, 101
Numbered Counting Board,
    1–20 (Reproducible 6), 37
Numbered Counting Board, 1–30
    (Reproducible 7), 37, 59
Numbered Counting Board, 1–50
    (Reproducible 8), 37, 59
number relationships
    going over 100, 153, 154
    Hippety Hop game, 133–141
    Race to 100 game, 142–149
numbers
    choosing, 8
    touching, 18
    two-digit, reading of, 7
number sense
    Number Chart Bingo!
        game, 97–101

progress, informal
    assessment of, 102
    of students, determining, 11

O

101 and Out! Assessment
    (Reproducible 23), 150
101 and Out! game, 150–160
101 and Out! Game Directions
    (Reproducible G-8R), 150, 156
101 and Out! Recording Sheet
    (Reproducible 22), 150
1–50 chart, 98
101–200 Chart (Reproducible C),
    150
one-digit numbers,
    differences of, 81–83
One More or Less lesson, 37–46
open number line, 175

P

pacing, 70
parentheses, use when recording, 71
partner games
    101 and Out!, 154
    Fill It Up!, 113–114
partners
    arrow clue practice with, 22
    assigning, 92
    discussion buddies, 135, 146, 152
    letting students choose, 92–93
    student-picked, 141
    talking with, 4–5
    working solo afterwards, 178
patterns, on hundreds chart, 55
place-value concept
    101 and Out! game, 150–160
    discussions on, 129–120
    Number Chart Bingo!
        game, 97–101
playing
    competitively, 115, 138
    games, at desks *vs.* floor, 93
    with partners, 154
    without sentence frames, 17
pocket hundreds chart, i–ii
pointing to numbers on
    Hundreds Chart, 23
posting directions, 153

practice options, 75
*Principles and Standards for School
    Mathematics* (NCTM), iii
projected hundreds chart, v
projection device, use of, 70
projection devices, use of, 67
puzzles. *See also Missing
    Number Puzzles* lesson

Q

question cards, modifying
    or omitting, 145

R

Race to 100: Action Cards Strips
    (Reproducible 20), 142
Race to 100: Five Strips
    (Reproducible 18), 142
Race to 100: Question Cards Strips
    (Reproducible 21), 142
Race to 100: Ten Strips
    (Reproducible 19), 142
Race to 100 game, 142–149
Race to 100 Game Directions
    (Reproducible G-7R),
    142
ranges of numbers, 104
reading, two-digit numbers, 7
recording
    different methods of, 136
    introduction of, 82–83
    methods of, 85
    open number line for, 175
    student's thinking, 149,
        171–172(figure)
recording sheets, use of, 96
repetition
    of game, 32
    importance of, 129
    strategies, 86
revoicing, 135
riddles. *See also Hundreds
    Chart Riddles* lesson
    advantages in using, 58, 64
    as formative assessment, 65
    vocabulary usage and, 65
    writing your own, 62–64
routines, 136
rows, for counting, 67

S

seating arrangements, for
    students, 15
second graders
    building the hundreds
        chart with, 11
    Number Chart Bingo!
        game, 97–101
    symbols and, 105
self-correction, 40
sentence frames
    introducing, 13
    playing without, 17
shortcuts, finding, 144
shuffling cards, 143
small groups
    games for, 124
    preparing materials for, 41
    working in, 145
Solving Comparison Problems
    lesson, 80–88
spinner, 38, 42
strategies for games,
    discussion of, 151
students
    finishing early, 88, 137, 166
    restlessness/fatigue of, 8
    seating arrangements, 15
student thinking
    examples of (*see under*
        specific lessons/games)
    giving time for, 17
    recording, during class
        discussions, 149
    representing using numbers
        and words, 171
subitizing, 67
subtraction
    connecting with addition, 87, 180
    Fill It Up! game, 111–116

finding differences (*See Solving
    Comparison Problems* lesson)
How Far Away? game, 173–180
The Larger Difference game,
    161–172
Race to 100 game, 142–149
    relationship to addition, 167
    student thinking about, 87
summary of lesson, 3, 4. *See
    also under specific lesson*
support, 30
symbols
    connecting to writing, 61, 105
    Race to 100 game, 142–149

T

teacher
    checklists for, 45–46, 56–57
    differentiating your instruction
        (*See under specific lessons*)
    reflections of (*see under
        specific lesson or game*)
    role of, 4–5
    what to do while students
        play games, 95
Teacher Checklist: *One More or
    One Less* (Reproducible 9),
    37, 45–46
Teacher Checklist: *Ten More or
    Ten Less* (Reproducible 10),
    37, 47, 56–57
teaching directions. *See under
    specific lesson or game*
ten, value of, 50
10-by-5 grid (Reproducible E),
    111
10-by-10 grid, in *Look, Quick!*
    lesson, 67
10-by-10 grid (Reproducible D),
    66, 114, 123, 124

Ten More or Ten Less lesson, 47–57
10×10 grid (bland Hundreds
    Chart)
    preparing, 114
thinking time, providing
    students with, 17
time requirements for lessons, 4.
    See also specific lessons
time savers, 9, 98, 100, 142,
    152
Too High, Too Low game,
    103–110
touching numbers,
    importance of, 18
turn taking, 94, 107
two-digit numbers
    adding and subtracting, 51
    differences of, 83–88
    reading, 7
Two High, Too Low Game
    Directions (Reproducible
    G-2R), 103, 108

U

*Using Math Talk to Help Students
    Learn* (Chapin), 135

V

visual support, for sentence
    frames, 13
vocabulary
    reviewing, 21
    riddles and, 65
    seeing and hearing, 99

W

winning, 95
writing, in math class, 155